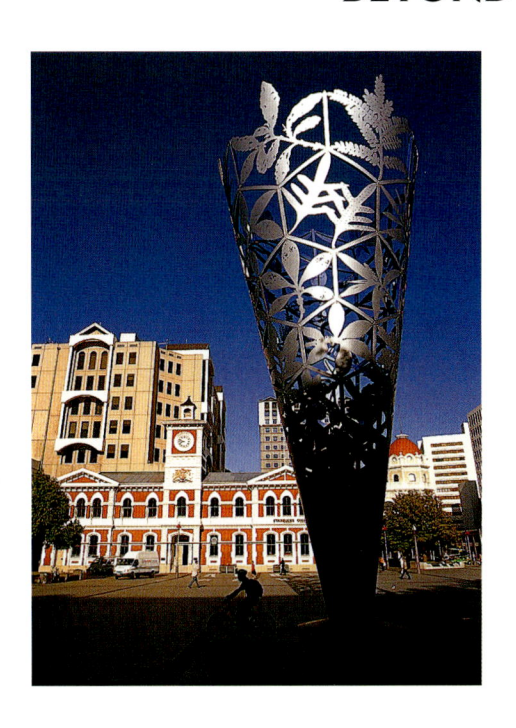

CHRISTCHURCH
and
BEYOND

CHRISTCHURCH
and BEYOND

Photography by David Wall

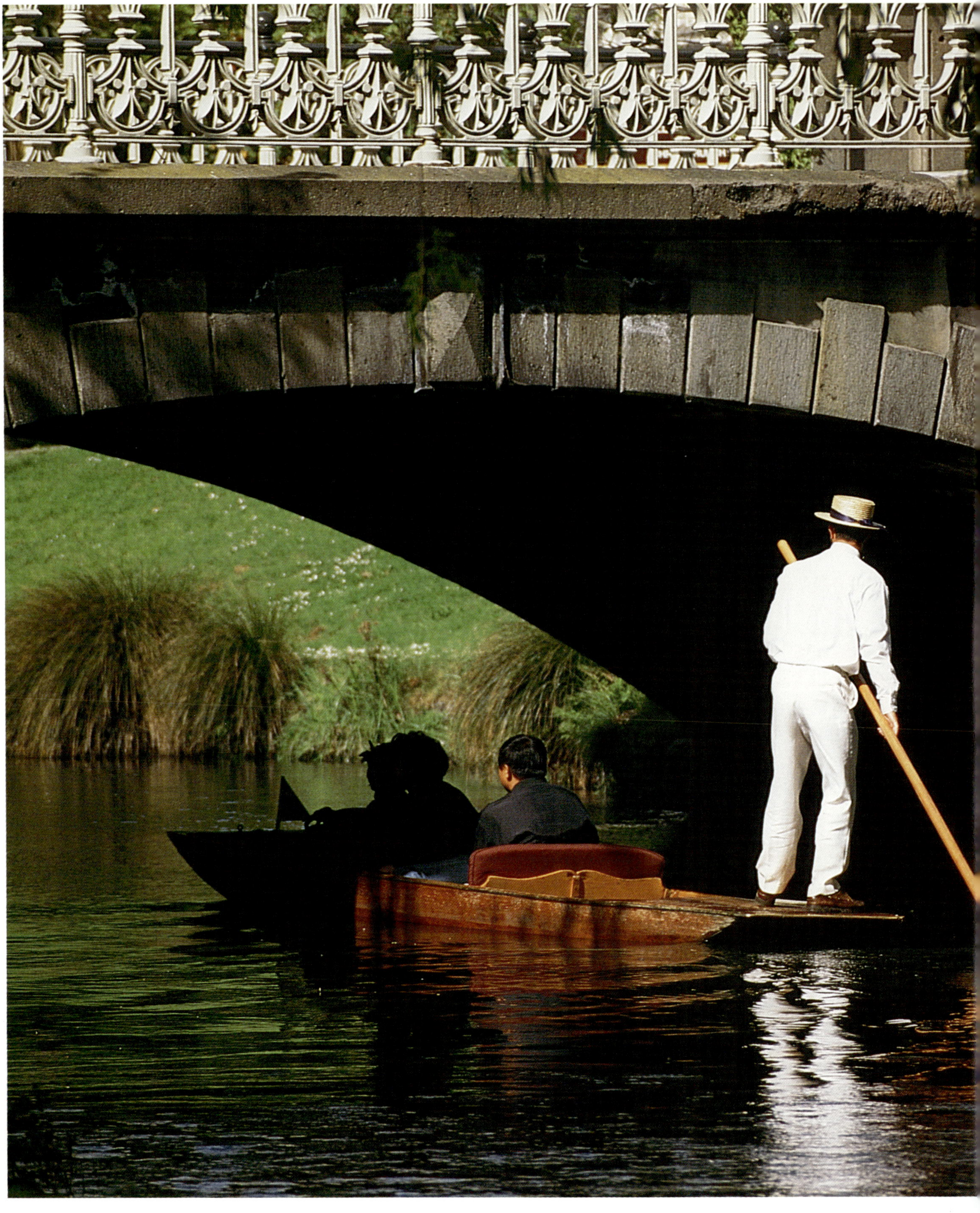

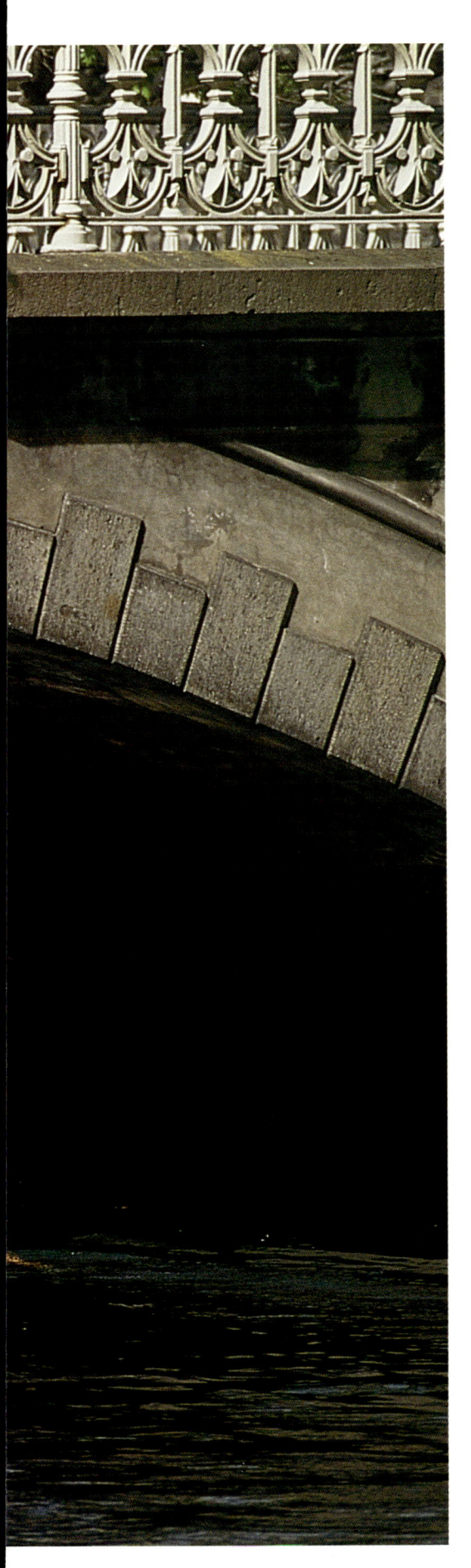

Introduction

Christchurch snuggles into the hills of the crater rim formed by the volcanic eruptions of millions of years ago and spills out onto the largest stretch of flat land in New Zealand, the Canterbury Plains.

A river idles its way through the city, heading eastward to the Pacific Ocean. Westward, beyond the plains, is a magnificent backdrop formed by the Southern Alps.

The city is the largest centre in the South Island and there are many things about it that speak of its English colonial past. In 1848 a group of Englishmen, many of whom were Church of England clerics, formed the Canterbury Association. Their dream was to establish a model Anglican colonial settlement. Early in the 1850s the first of these European settlers arrived by sailing ship. From the port they had to walk up and over the crater hills with all their possessions and down to the swampland on the plain – a considerable distance.

Out of this challenging beginning has grown a delightful, modern city. But its charming older buildings, many built of stone in a neo-Gothic style, remind us of those resilient pioneers and their dream. One of their most precious gifts has been the spacious park with its beautiful trees and Botanic Gardens that are so close to the centre of Christchurch.

These were not, however, the first people to live in the area. Maori were the tangata whenua – the people of the land. As now, there were far fewer Maori in the South Island than in the North and they had settled largely in coastal areas. So too did the earliest Europeans, whalers who hunted in these seas; in the bays of the harbour, along the coast and around Banks Peninsula there are fascinating remnants of these first settlements.

Punting on the Avon

The prosperity of the region has always had farming as its foundation. The plains, covered with native tussock, were relatively easily adapted for running sheep and growing crops. Of course these days there's a much greater diversity of farming, including a very buoyant wine industry. Sipping one's way along the region's wine trails is an increasingly popular pastime!

There is a huge range of activities on offer in Canterbury. The Southern Alps offer some of the most challenging mountaineering in the world, along with skiing. There's fishing in the lakes and rivers, as well as kayaking and jet-boating, camping and tramping, sailing and windsurfing; and lazing about on the beach. Indeed, there's almost any outdoor pleasure you can think of. Added to this, Canterbury and Christchurch have always attracted artists and craftspeople. What more could anyone want?

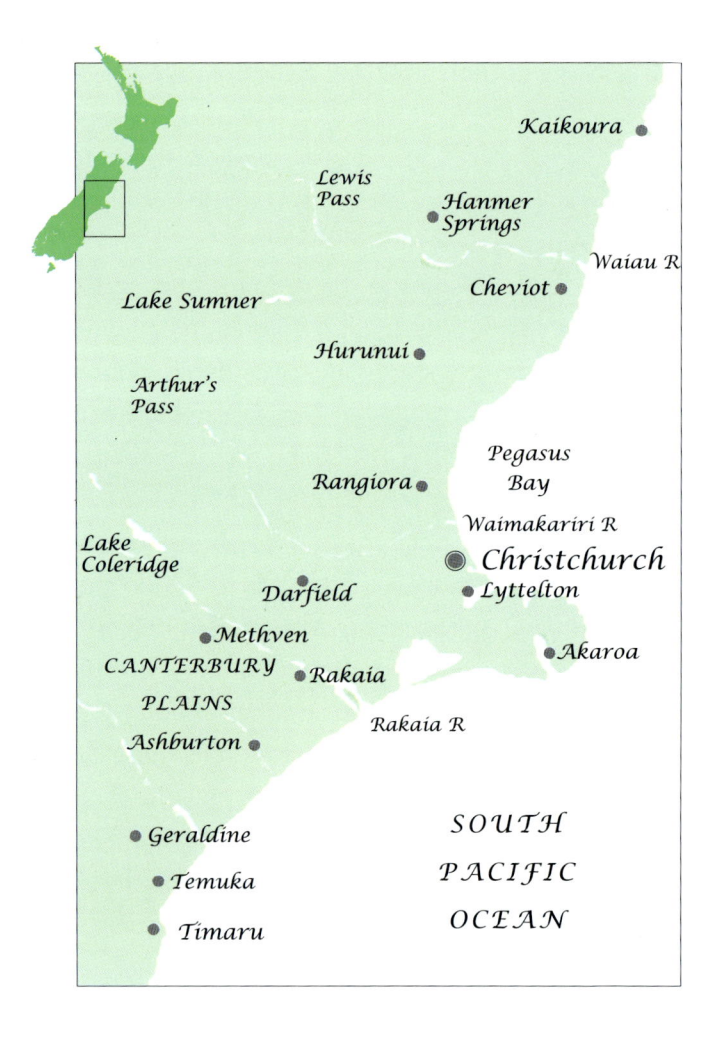

The River Avon is one of the defining elements of this gentle, southern city. It's at its most charming as it wends its way through central Christchurch, alongside rows of stately trees just a few metres away from the roar of the traffic – the perfect setting for a sunny autumn stroll.

Captain James Cook was one of the great European explorers of the Pacific. He made three voyages to New Zealand but his first sighting was on 7 October 1769. As commander of the *Endeavour*, Cook was charged with investigating 'the presence of any continental land mass in the Southern Pacific Ocean'. He sailed round this 'new' land over the next six months and charted the coastline with remarkable accuracy. This statue of Cook can be found in Victoria Square.

Queen Victoria was on the British throne when, on her behalf, Governor William Hobson claimed sovereignty over New Zealand. Therefore, throughout New Zealand there's no shortage of place names and statues in honour of that grand monarch and Christchurch is no exception. Victoria Square features a statue of the queen and also boasts a working floral clock (one of the earliest in the world).

The Canterbury Association made provision in their plan for a Grammar School for boys, along the lines of the prestigious public schools of England. Christ's College is still seen as one of New Zealand's best private schools. It opened its first classroom in 1857 and its early stone buildings and quadrangles firmly state its English heritage. The pupils' straw boaters and humbug-striped blazers also speak of the school's history. That there has been such a long-lasting English influence is not surprising given that of the first 13 headmasters, 12 were graduates of either Oxford or Cambridge University.

11

One of the first and most enterprising of the European settler families in Canterbury was that of brothers William and John Deans. They had grown up in the parish of Riccarton, Ayrshire, in south-west Scotland and settled in this province in 1843. It was they who named the river, seen above, after the Ayrshire Avon.

Even allowing for the Canterbury Association's plan, it was a natural instinct for the settlers to look back to their homelands, not necessarily to try to recreate where they came from, but perhaps to have some reminders, such as their own Oxford Terrace, Cambridge Terrace and the pubs (above) by the banks of the river.

The Canterbury 'Pilgrims' arrived in 1850 with the aim of building a model colonial settlement – with, of course, its own cathedral. The foundation stone was laid in 1864 and the Gothic-style Cathedral Church of Christ was completed in 1904. In 2000, to mark the new millennium, as well as the city's 150th anniversary, artist Neil Dawson was commissioned to create a public work of art. His *Chalice*, featuring native leaf patterns cut out of sheet aluminium, stands 18m high in Cathedral Square.

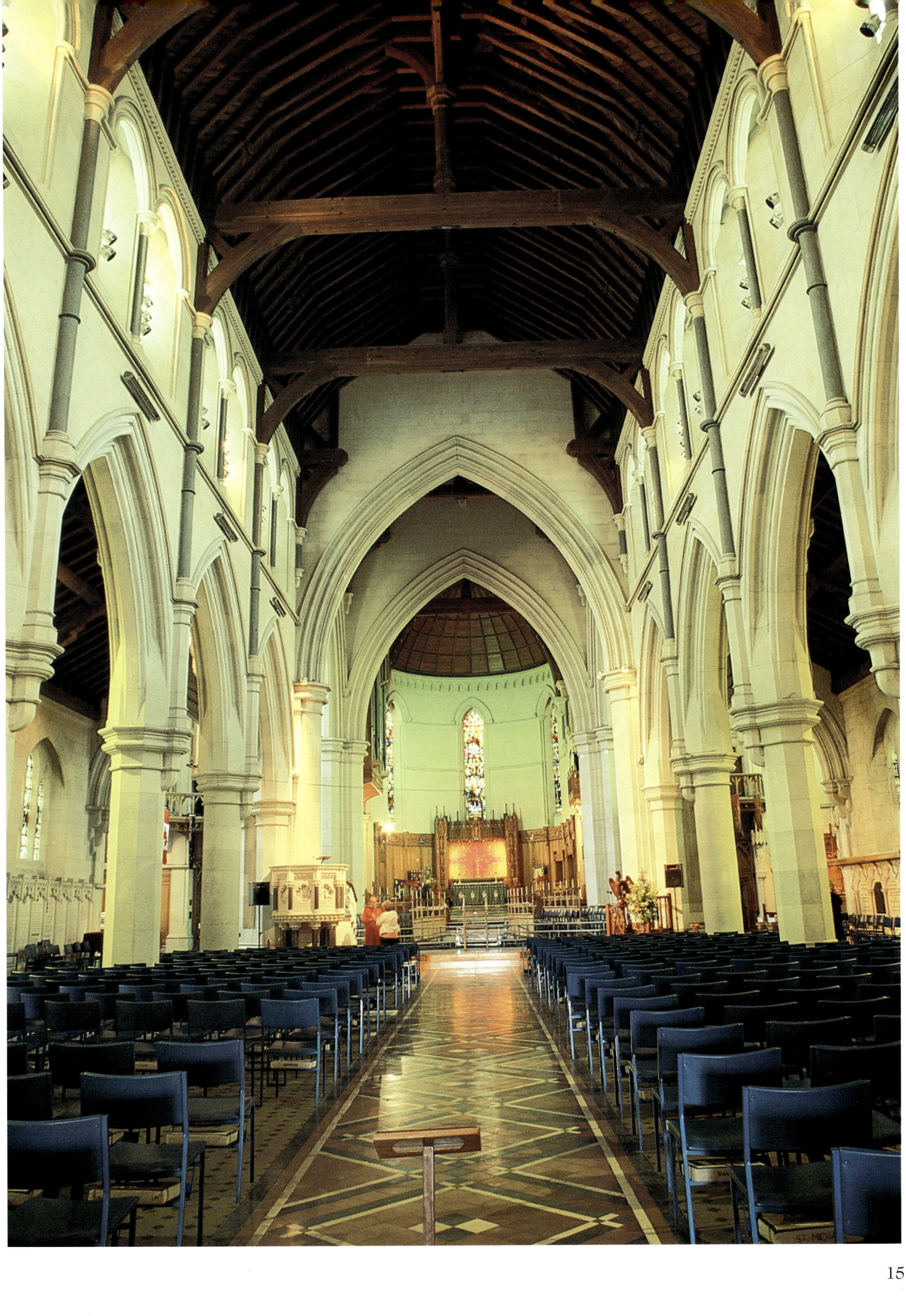

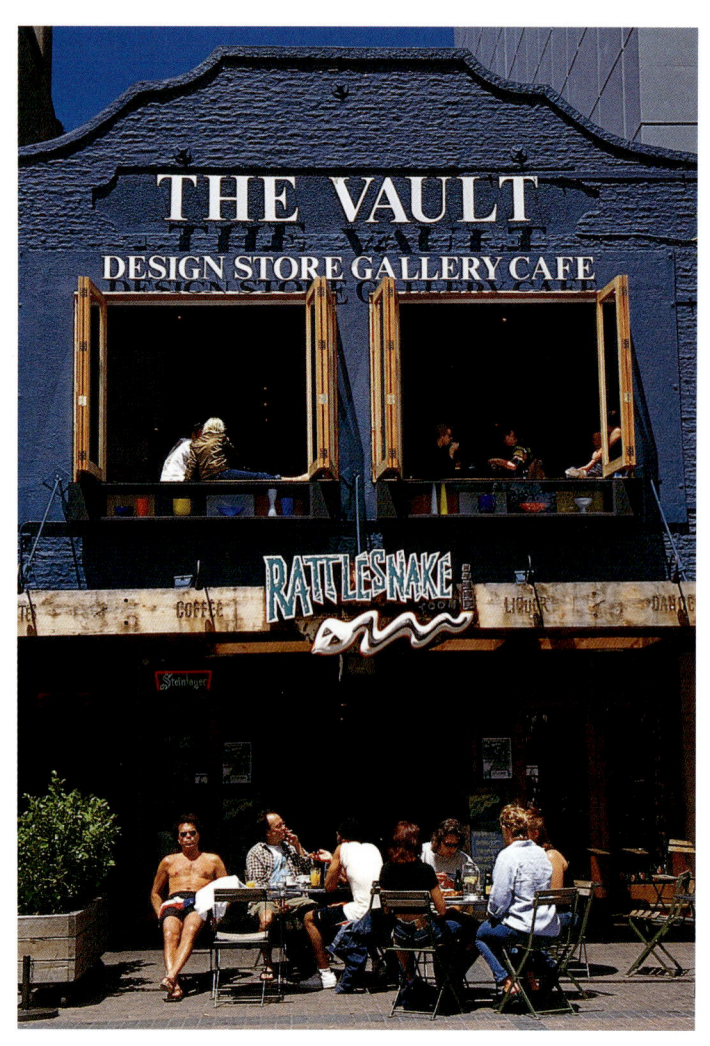

Christchurch has embraced the concept of the 'café society' with great enthusiasm. Cafés and wine bars can be found in all corners of the city, and particularly in the city centre. Whether it's latte or cappuccino, herbal tea or a glass of wine that you fancy, you'll find it in the pedestrian precinct of the City Mall. And just round the corner from the mall is Oxford Terrace (above). Stroll alongside the river and look across to 'The Strip', a row almost exclusively made up of cafés snuggled together with their pavement tables and umbrellas, seen here on the right.

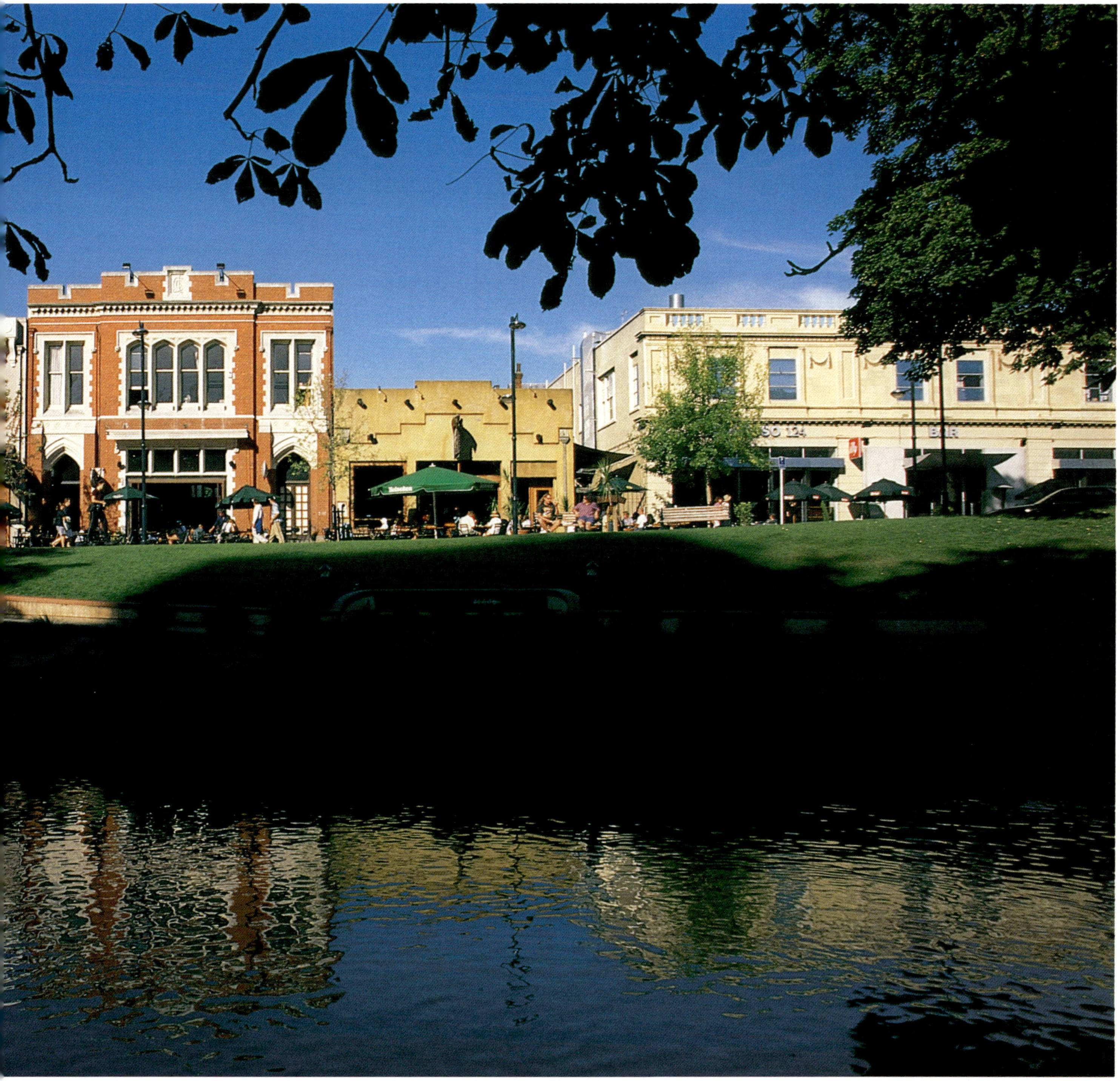

The floodlit Canterbury Provincial Council Chambers make an imposing city sight. From 1852 New Zealand was divided into provincial districts, each with its governing superintendent and 12-man council. The only surviving purpose-built provincial government complex is the charming collection of stone and timber buildings that served Canterbury. It was first used by the council in September 1859. Built in the style of the High Victorian Gothic Revival, extensive use was made of local materials. The different types of stone came from various parts of the province and the beautiful timbers used in the interior are native kauri and rimu.

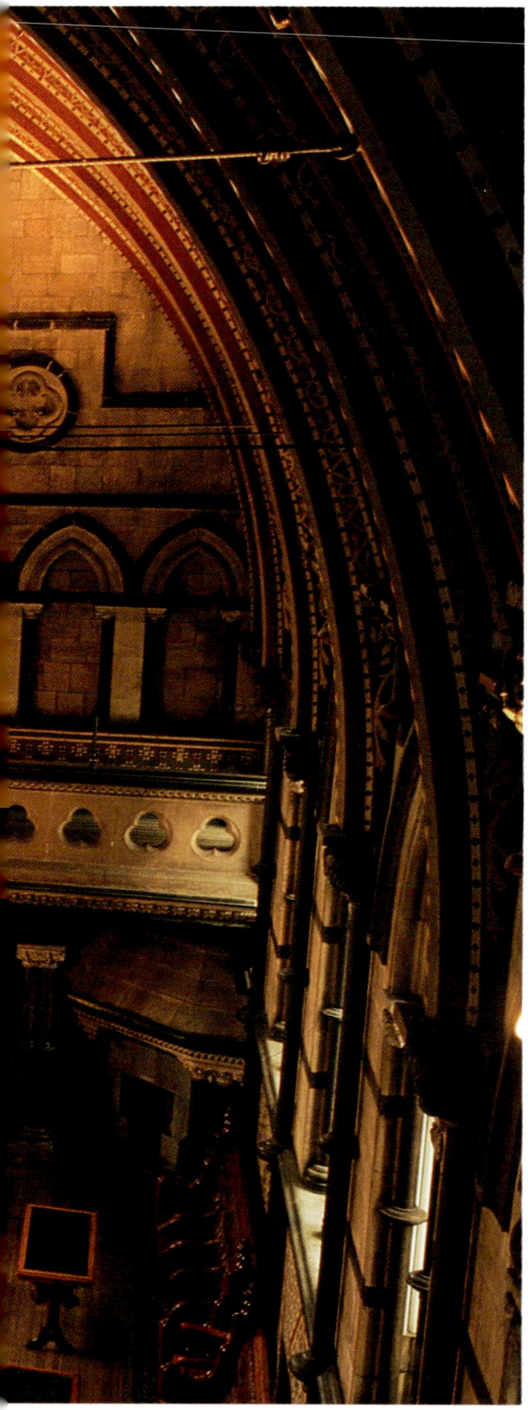

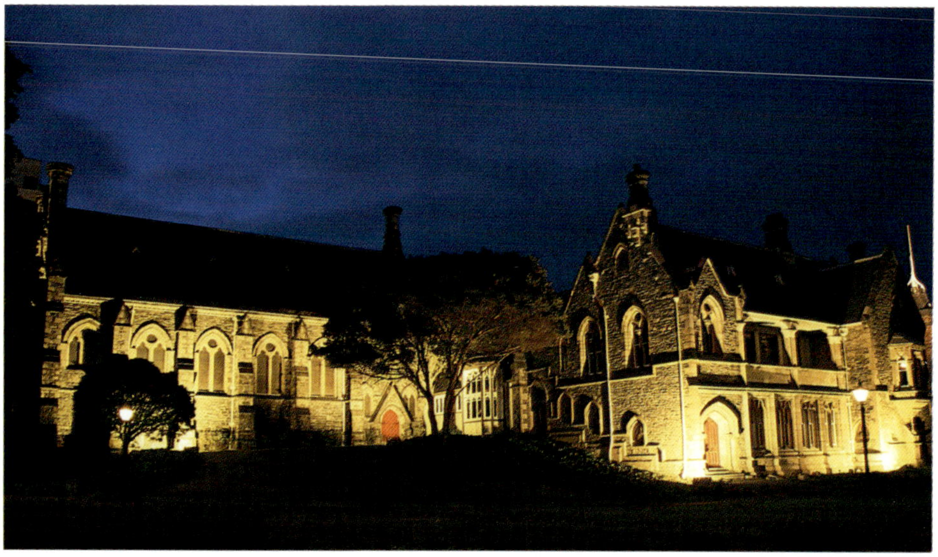

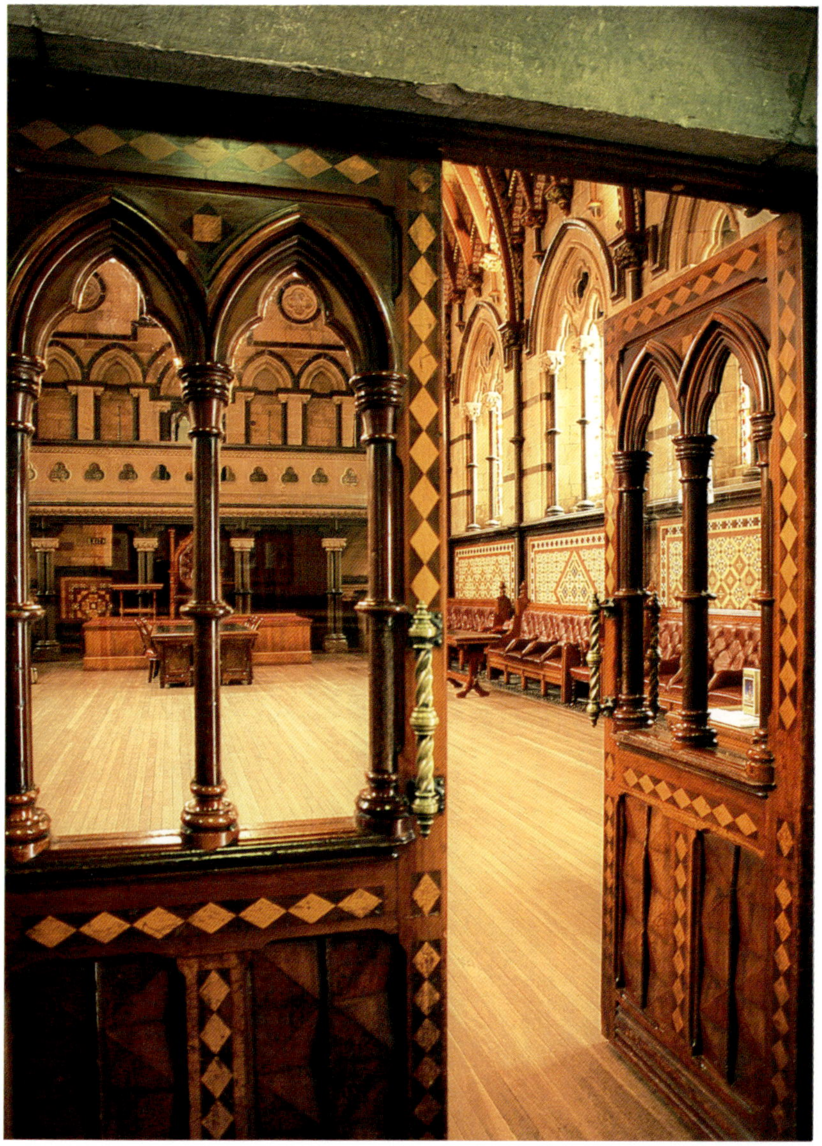

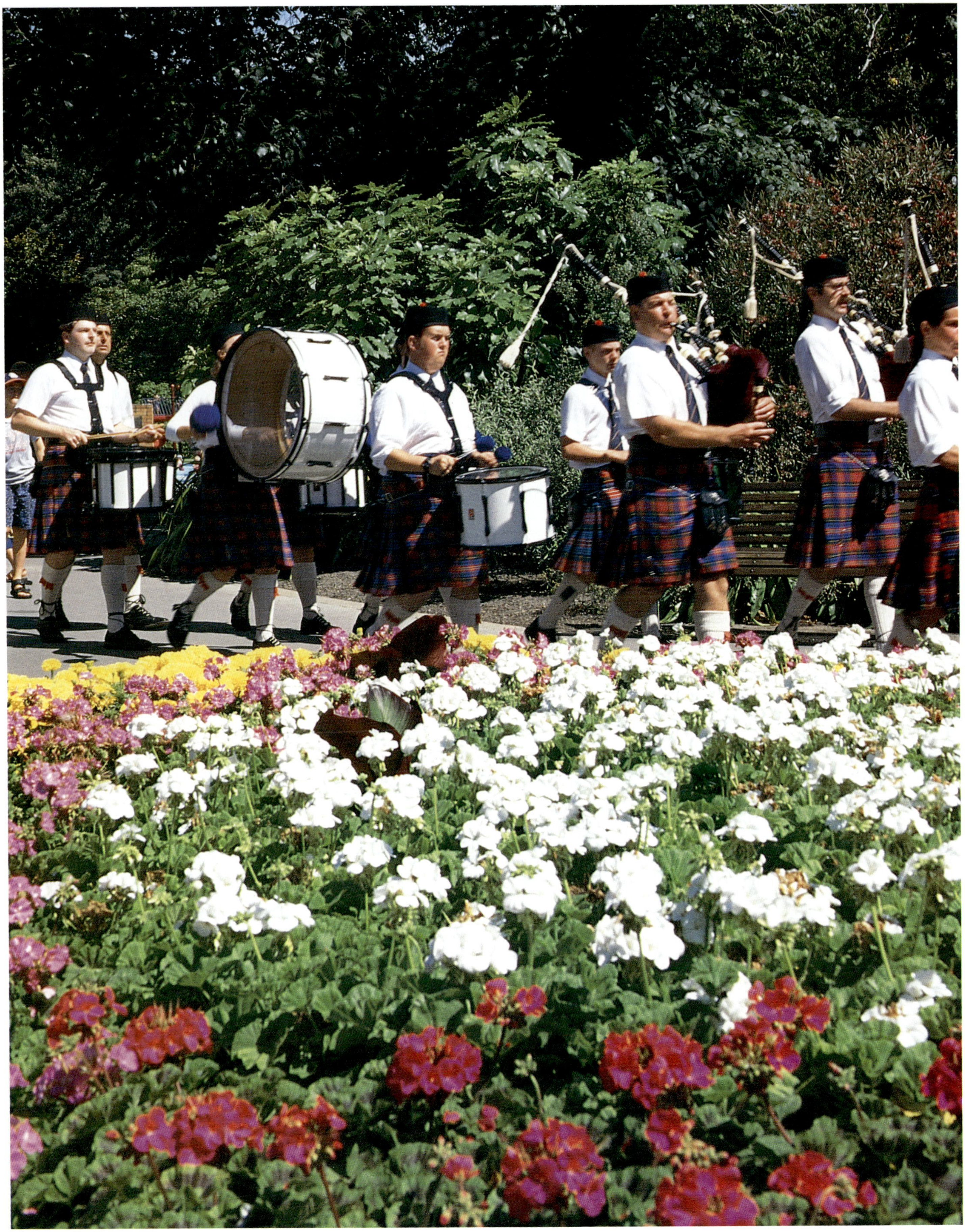

The time of European settlement in New Zealand was also an age of great scientific exploration. As well as Hagley Park, the founders of the Canterbury Association set aside a 30-hectare expanse in which to plant introduced species alongside native plants. The swamp and tussock they found on their arrival also contained rich alluvial soil in which plants could flourish. For lovers or joggers, visitors or locals, and even devotees of the pipe band, today the Botanic Gardens are a much enjoyed treasure of the city.

No matter what time of the year, Hagley Park is a gift greatly treasured by locals. There's something quite magical about a walk around Hagley Park on a crisp winter's morning or a sunny summer's afternoon. It provides a wonderful expanse of greenery in the middle of the city and to a large extent the motorcar has been kept at bay! Two major avenues have been conceded over the years, allowing car access into the city centre and dividing the park into three components: North, South and Little Hagley. Further incursions have been fiercely resisted.

Trees were planted around the perimeter and provide natural avenues for the many walkers, cyclists and joggers in the community. The park is also a major sporting venue: how many cities have a golf course at their centre? With its tennis courts, rugby fields, cricket pitches, netball courts, and occasional open-air concerts, Hagley Park is a much used amenity.

Overleaf: Subsequent generations can only admire the foresight of those early European settlers in their decision to set aside land for Hagley Park and the Botanic Gardens, seen here with the city centre and suburbs stretching to the Pacific Ocean.

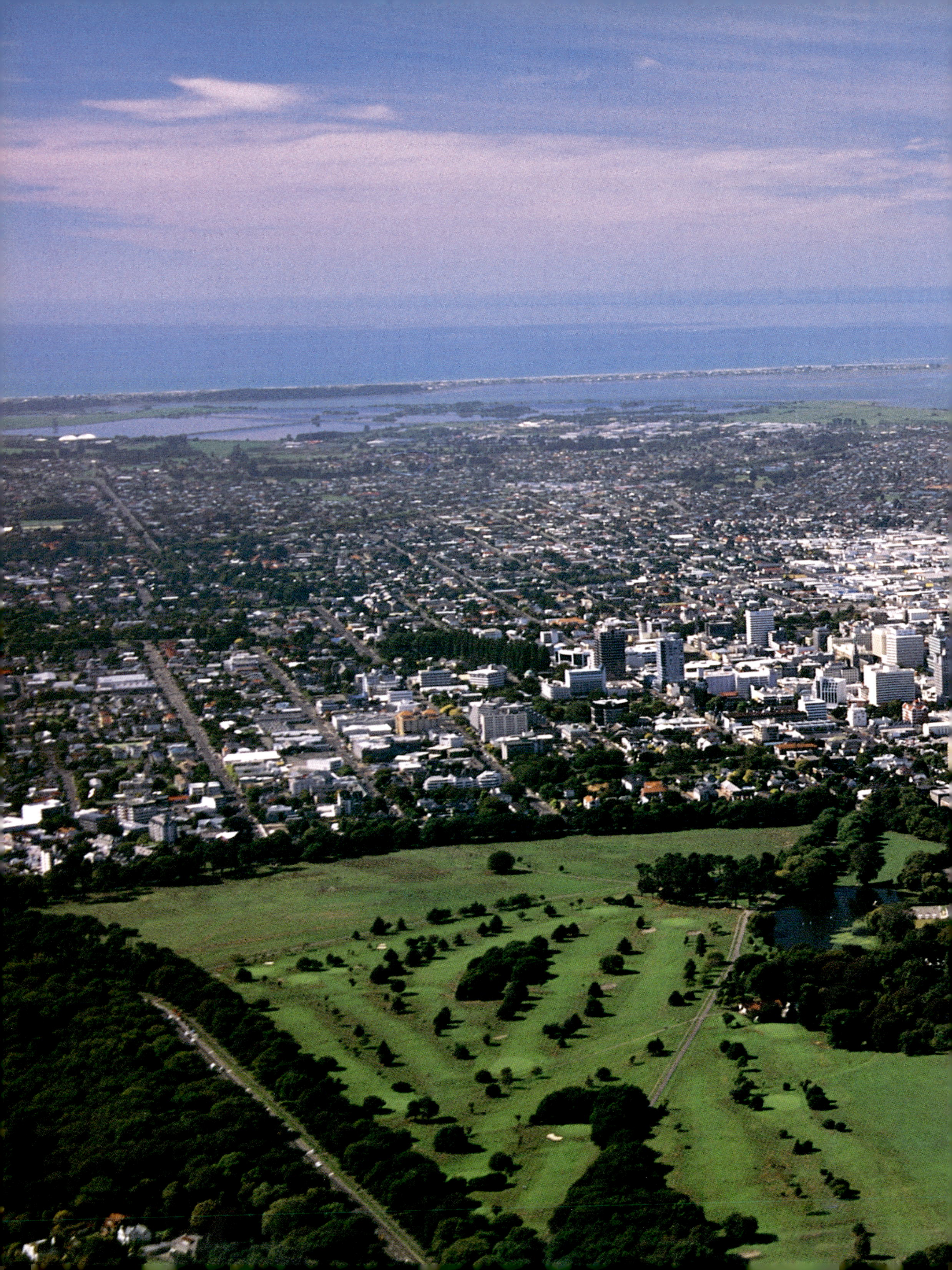

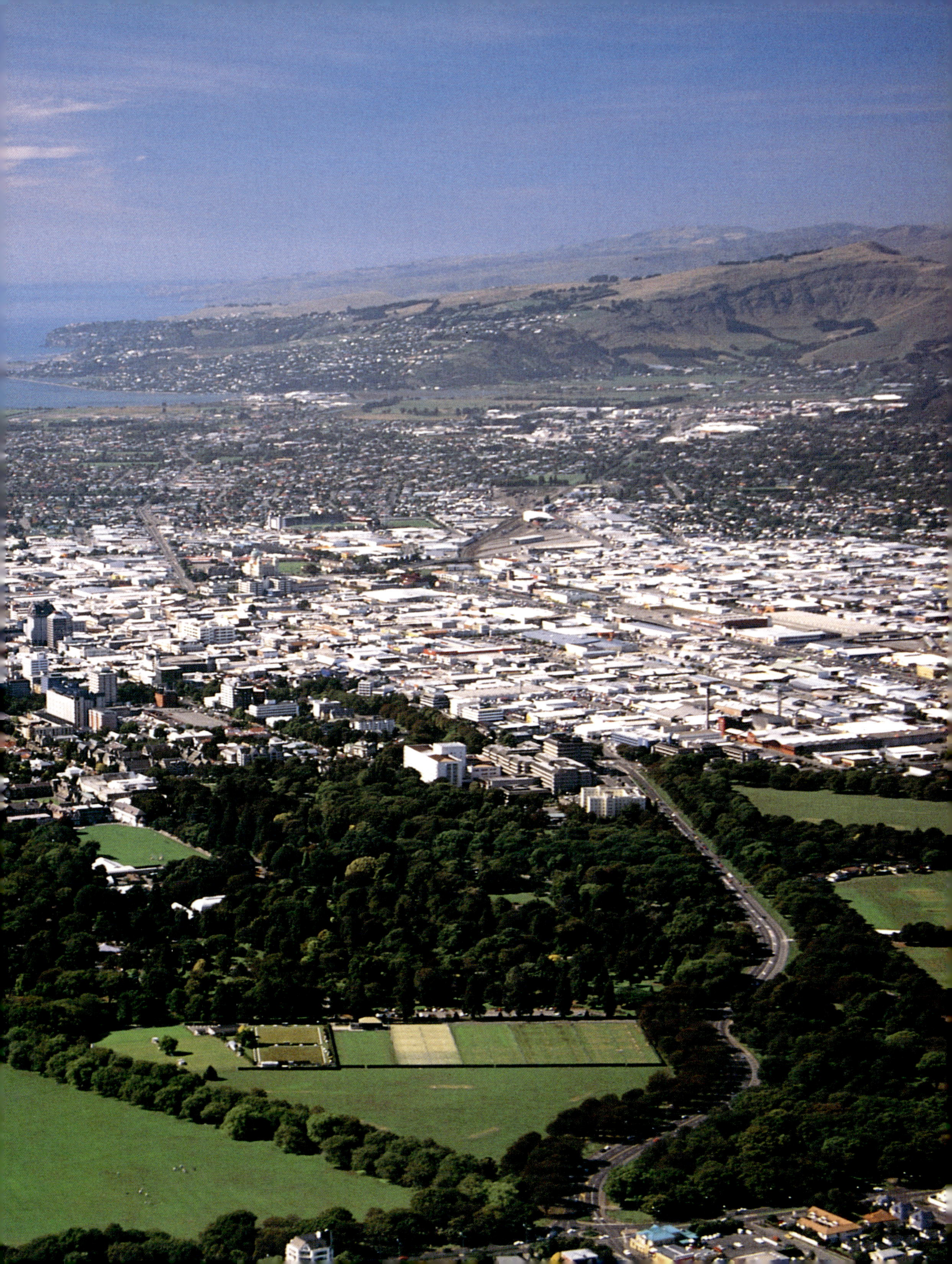

26

In at least nine out of 12 months of the year Christchurch has a festival. Visitors and locals alike love the sense of energy these events bring. Interests in arts, jazz, adventure, food and wine, books and flowers are all catered for. The city is the venue for the World Buskers Festival, which attracts fire jugglers (left) among its many astonishing acts. Christchurch was the first city in the world to have a Festival of Romance.

The Roman Catholic settlers decided on a High Renaissance style for their basilica, the Cathedral of the Blessed Sacrament. Whether it is lit at night or when in the day its domes stand proud against a clear Canterbury sky, it is a very striking building.

One of the leading figures of the Canterbury Association, John Robert Godley, arrived with his family in 1850 at Port Cooper (later named Lyttelton Harbour). He was a most influential figure in the first few years of the Canterbury settlement. A number of geographical features in Canterbury were named after him, including Godley Head, a high clump of rocky crags on the northern side of the entrance to the Harbour. Godley's statue — the first to be erected in New Zealand — can be seen in Cathedral Square, facing the front doors of the Anglican Cathedral.

For Maori a 'marae' is a place for the community to meet. A place of great spiritual and cultural importance often containing a meeting house with carvings, weaving and Maori art, it also includes a courtyard area for people to gather. Nga Hau E Wha National Marae, 10 minutes from the centre of Christchurch, is one of the largest in New Zealand and contains two spectacularly carved meeting houses. The name means 'Marae of the Four Winds', in other words a place where people from all points of the compass are welcome.

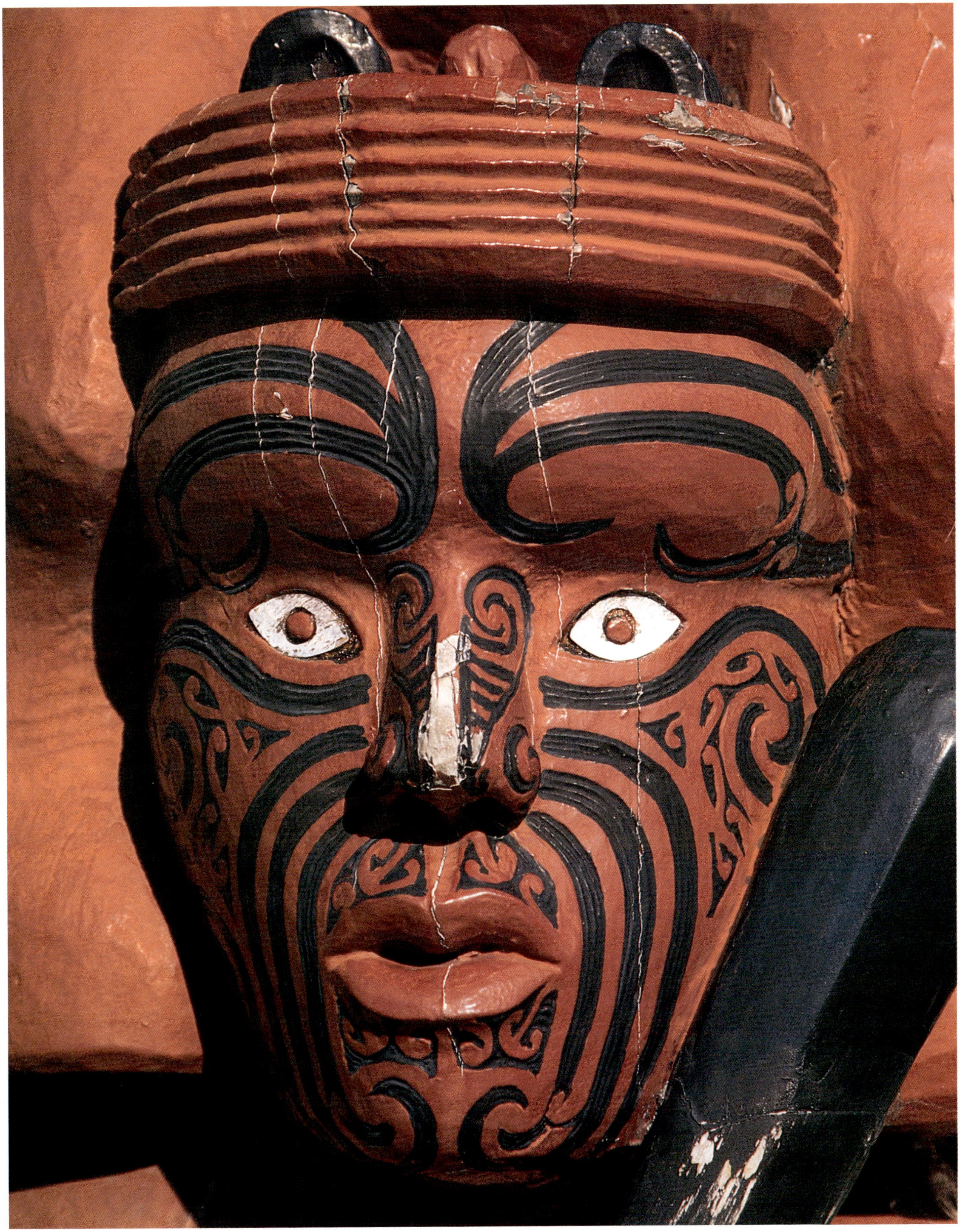

32

Cathedral Square provides a pedestrian sanctuary in the heart of the city where flower and fruit sellers offer their wares. Other craftspeople set up stalls on market days and there's often some form of entertainment. After many years of going it alone, the Christchurch Wizard (left) has now been recognised as a living work of art by the City Council; during the warm months of the year he can usually be found on his stepladder entertaining lunchtime strollers with his particular philosophy of living. Sometimes he has competition!

The style of boats may have changed over the years but the historic Antigua Boatsheds have been doing business since 1882. The gentle, meandering 'stream' – as the River Avon was referred to in many early accounts of the city – lends itself to a leisurely row, or an even more leisurely punt. Kayak, canoe or punt, the ducks seem happy to tolerate these intruders into their domain.

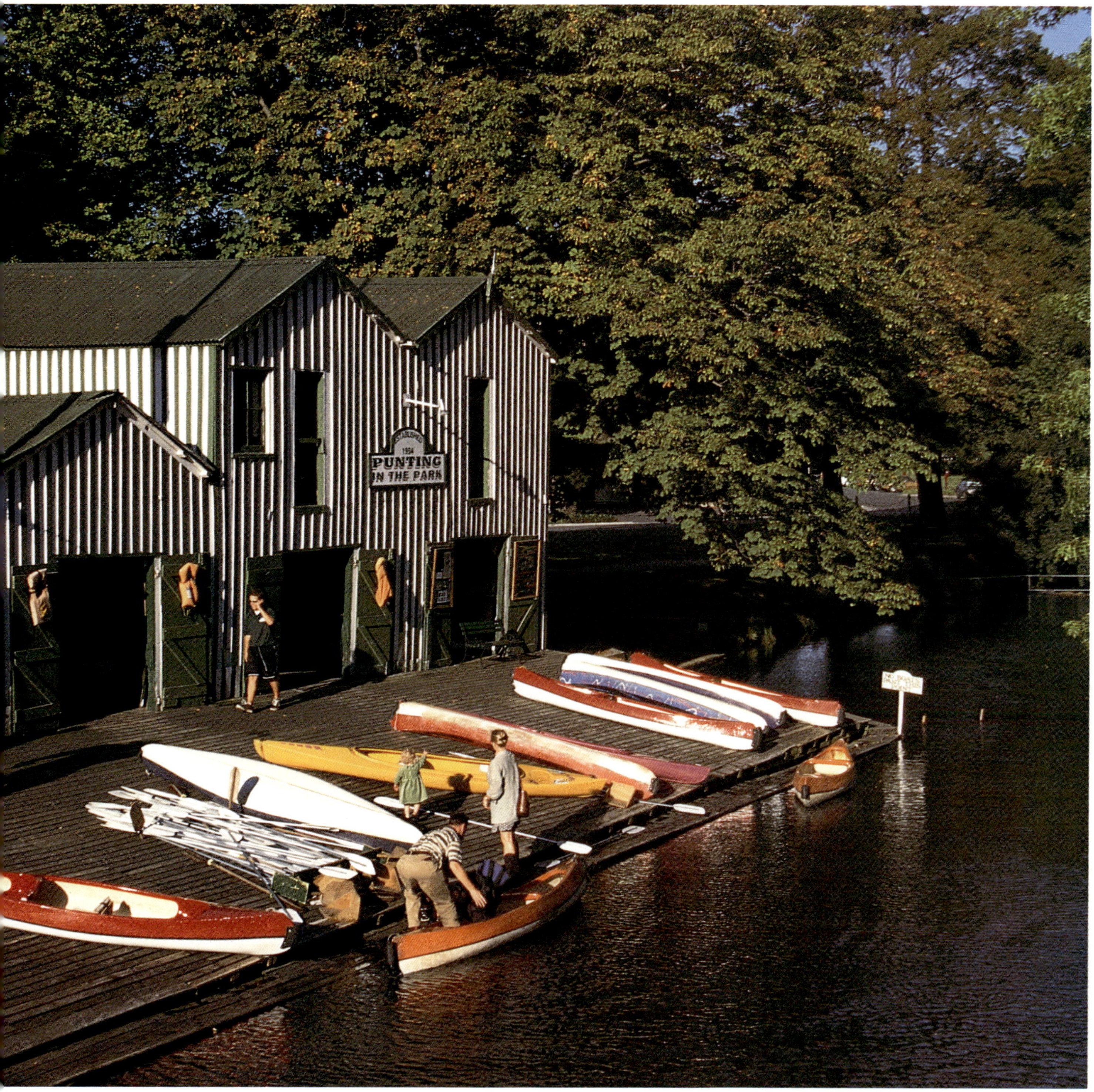
1994
PUNTING
IN THE PARK

The Yaldhurst Museum of Transport and Science, only 12 kilometres from the city centre, is a must for anyone interested in aspects of vintage transport, including the horse and cart, Model-T Fords, motor cycles, racing cars or fire engines.

Are the space explorers of today any more intrepid than those of the late 19th century who crossed the Southern Alps in a horse-drawn cart?

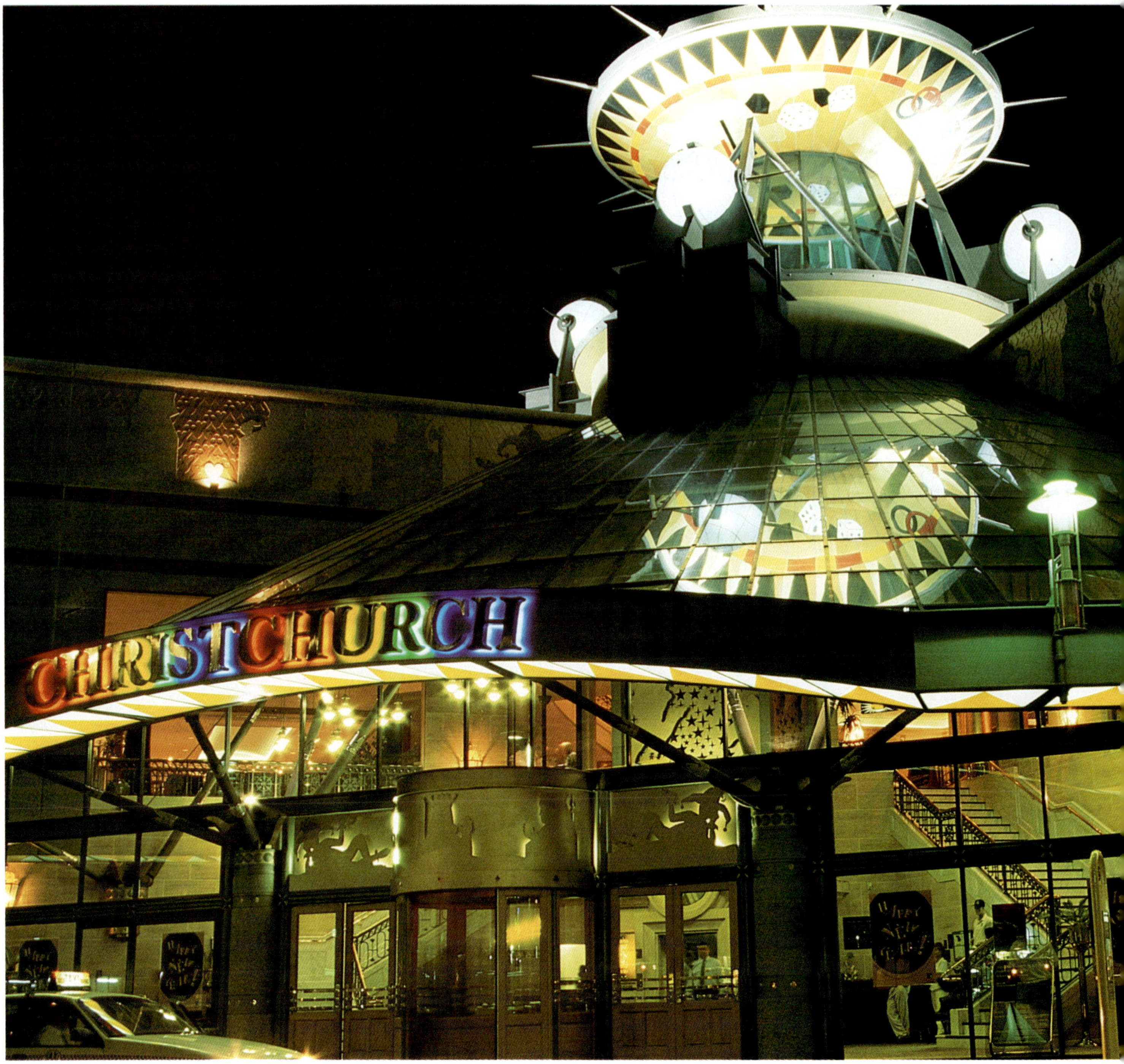
CHRISTCHURCH

Topped with a larger-than-life roulette wheel, the Christchurch Casino (left) lights its corner of the city at night. Close to Victoria Square and the Town Hall, it provides 36 gaming tables and 428 pokie machines to get the adrenalin going at any time of the day or night.

Overleaf: One of the most delightful gardens of this Garden City is located only five minutes from the city centre. First developed just before the turn of the 20th century the property with its fine homestead was originally known as 'Karewa'. In 1905 its new owner renamed it 'Mona Vale' after her mother's birthplace in Tasmania. In the 1960s the community found it had a fight on its hands – to save this historic building from being demolished and its beautiful grounds from being subdivided. Thanks to individual and civic generosity, Mona Vale is now a public treasure.

39

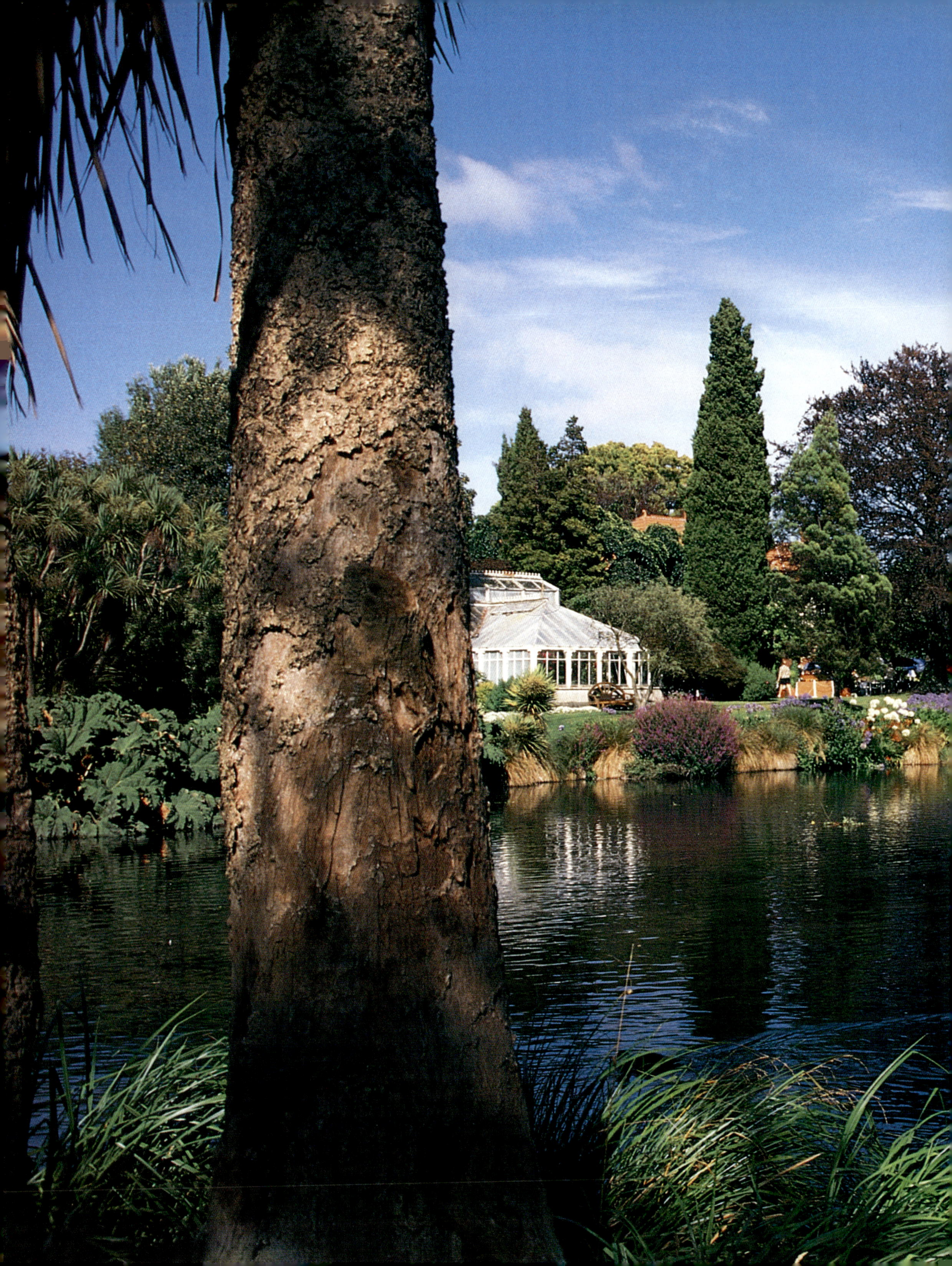

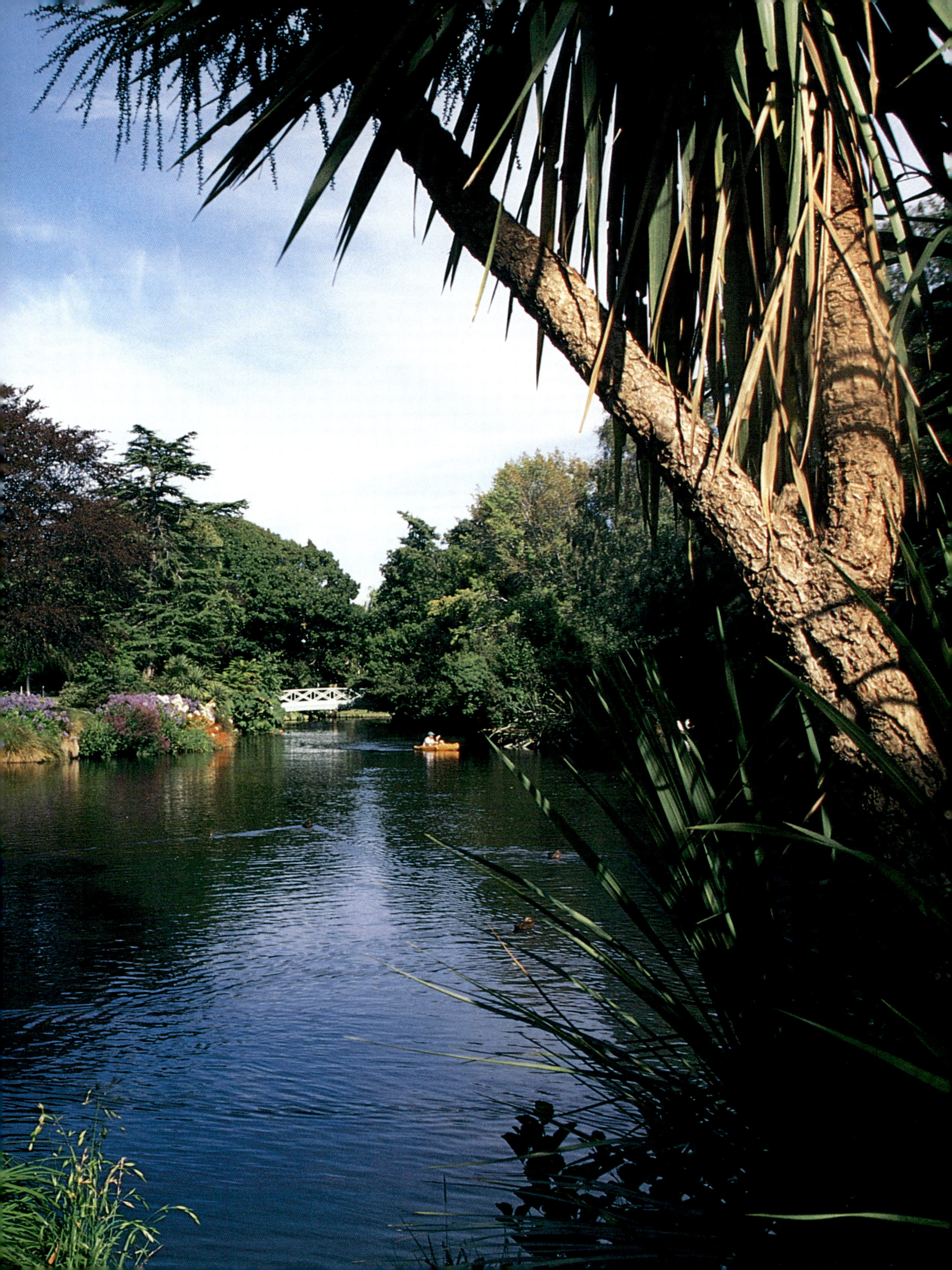

Visitors can wander round the five and half hectares of gardens and lawn that comprise Mona Vale. The River Avon meanders through the grounds, and there is no shortage of plump ducks to take your bread! Mona Vale is especially worth a visit to see the iris and rose gardens.

On the site of the old herb garden at Mona Vale is now a small garden structure with colourful stained glass doors.

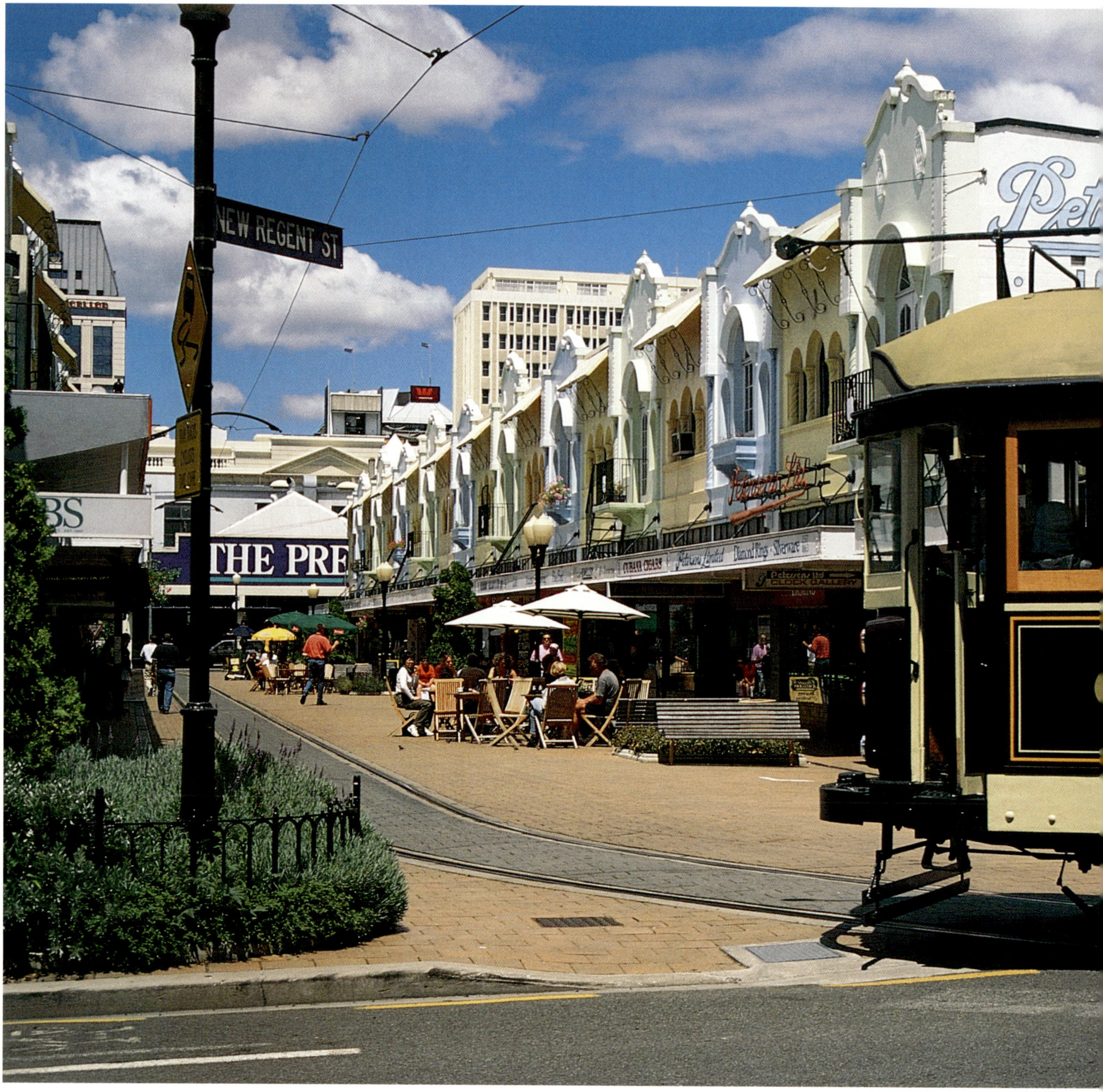
NEW REGENT ST

In 1954 the electric trams that were so much a part of the city's transport system gave way to the bus and the motorcar. The enthusiasts of the Historical Tramway Society rescued and restored the few trams that survived, and in 1995 they returned, bringing their old-world charm to the streets once more. The trams run a loop through the central city, taking in the Arts Centre, Victoria Square and New Regent Street. The latter is unique in Christchurch with its art deco architectural influence; the street has an inviting atmosphere all of its own and you can always get a fine cup of coffee in one of the many cafés.

46

Christchurch's historic links to England are very much apparent in the Arts Centre, with its charming neo-Gothic buildings and its town crier. This thriving, energetic complex of cafés, artists' studios, art galleries, theatres and cinemas was originally the home of the University of Canterbury – or Canterbury University College as it was named when established in 1873, and at which Ernest Lord Rutherford was an early scholar. The den in which the 'Father of the Atom' did his early experiments can still be visited. When the university moved to its present suburban site in the 1960s, these historic buildings were gifted to the city.

On its journey round the city loop, the tram runs down Worcester Boulevard with the Arts Centre on its left and the fine old buildings of the Canterbury Museum at the end of the street. The museum opened in 1870 under the directorship of Dr Julius von Haast, the distinguished explorer who was also the provincial geologist – and whose idea it was to build the museum.

Te Puna o Waiwhetu, Christchurch's new art gallery, was designed by The Buchan Group and opened in May 2003. Fronted by curving walls of glass and metal, the building is the largest art institution in the South Island. It features two floors of exhibition space, as well as a Sculpture Garden and a café and wine bar.

pacTrust GO Canterbury!
Ford
Team Hutchinson Ford
Coca-Cola

Canterbury is as passionate and parochial about its rugby football as any other province in New Zealand. Not only do the fans adorn themselves in the local team colours of red and black – even the city's public waste bins get striped when there's a big match in town, like this Canterbury Crusaders v. Wellington Hurricanes battle in the Super 12 Rugby series. Rugby followers the world over will know Jade Stadium, though they may be more familiar with its previous name of 'Lancaster Park'.

The International Antarctic Centre is literally round the corner from Christchurch Airport. Admirable international co-operation exists among scientists at Antarctica and this complex houses the New Zealand, United States and Italian Antarctic Research Programmes.

The complex has a Visitor Centre (above) where you can slide down a snow slope (left), feel the icy wind-chills of those extreme southern latitudes or explore a snow cave. It is as close as most of us will get to the snow and ice experience of that awesome continent!

There is still something magical about flight, even after a century in which we've advanced from Tiger Moth to Concorde. One of the earliest airbases in the country, the old RNZAF Base at Wigram, about 20 minutes' drive from the city centre, is now home to Air Force World. It's a great place to experience some of that magic among the 28 beautifully restored classic aircraft in its collection. These old aircraft are imaginatively displayed in realistic settings.

55

The gentle, questing llama and the handsome pukeko (right) are not natural neighbours but exotic combinations are not unusual at Willowbank Wildlife Reserve. The philosophy of Willowbank, on the outskirts of Christchurch, is to create as spacious and as natural an environment as possible for its extensive native and introduced wildlife collection. It contains many of New Zealand's rare nocturnal animals and birds, including the bashful kiwi. If you go quietly, it is quite possible to catch a glimpse of New Zealand's national bird.

57

Keeping the Pacific Ocean at bay, the South New Brighton spit is very close to the city and yet, if a solitary stroll is what one is after, it offers plenty of scope.

The suburb of New Brighton was named after the seaside town in England. Further along this beach, closer to the main shopping area, is the recently built New Brighton pier. It's become a popular fishing spot and it's always been a favourite of surfies; even in winter their black wetsuits can be seen bobbing in the swell as they wait for just the right combination of force and foam.

58

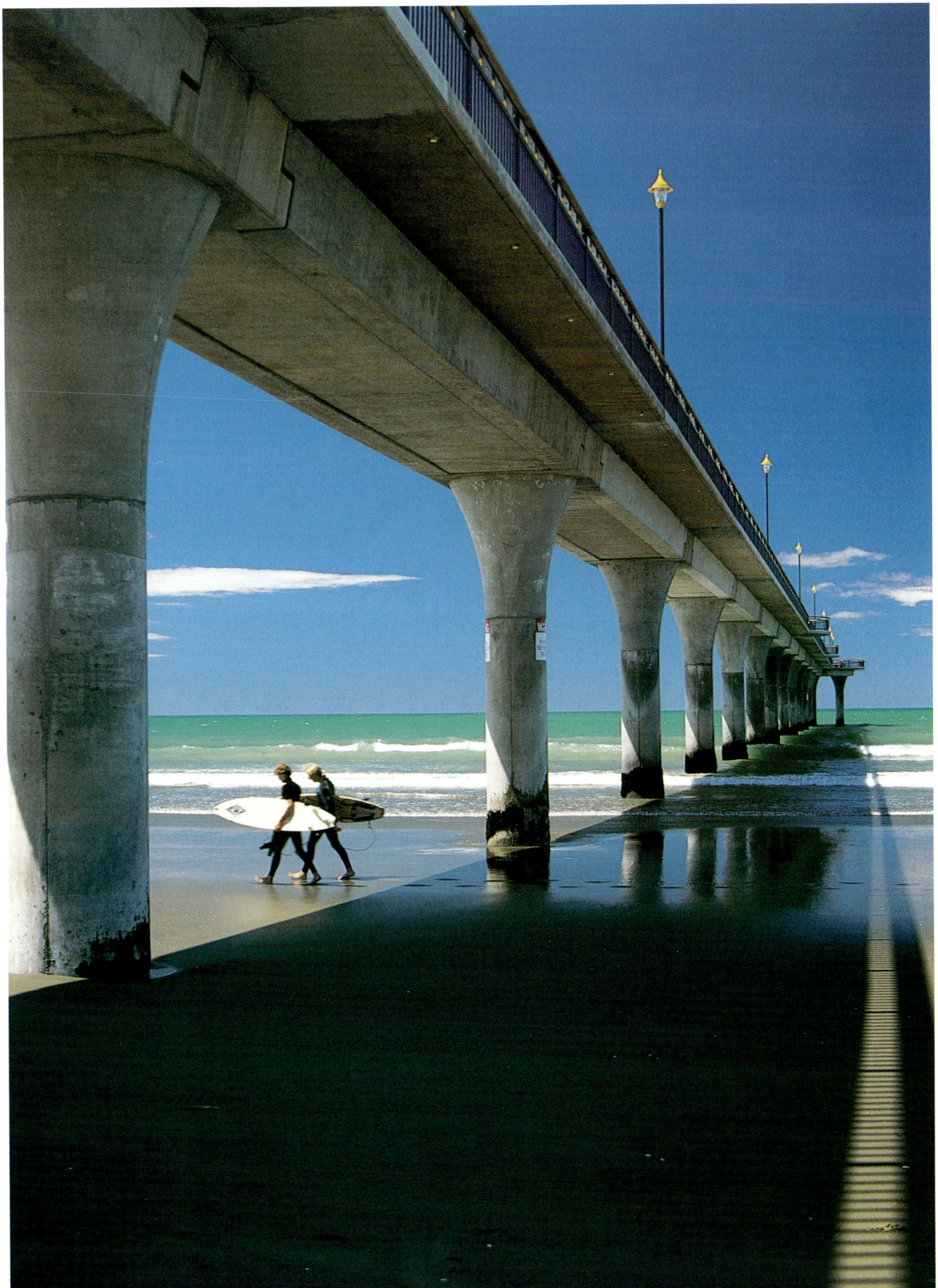

If bobbing on the ocean isn't your thing, New Brighton can offer you a ride in a Bungee Rocket. At 160 kilometres an hour – 50 metres high in one second – that's about 5Gs of gravity, followed by weightlessness, followed by 'ground rush': and that happens about 10 times per ride!

Across the water is another bay – Sumner. The striking, isolated outcrop of rock on the foreshore is 11 metres high. It was called by Maori 'Tuawera' or 'burnt rock' and was an ancient burial site for the Waitaha people. Today it's known as Cave Rock.

Sumner, nestled in a valley sheltered by hills, is an increasingly sought-after suburb with a sunnier, milder climate than the central areas of Christchurch. Sumner never became quite the bustling centre the early European settlers thought it would because of access difficulties in those days – Christchurch could only be reached by boat or over rocks!

Sumner Head provides a great vantage point where you can watch the ships on the horizon or gaze at the distant Southern Alps beyond the plains. There's a scenic walk around Sumner Head which is also a very popular area for hang-gliding – adventure romance of a different kind as the colourful gliders dip and soar with the thermals.

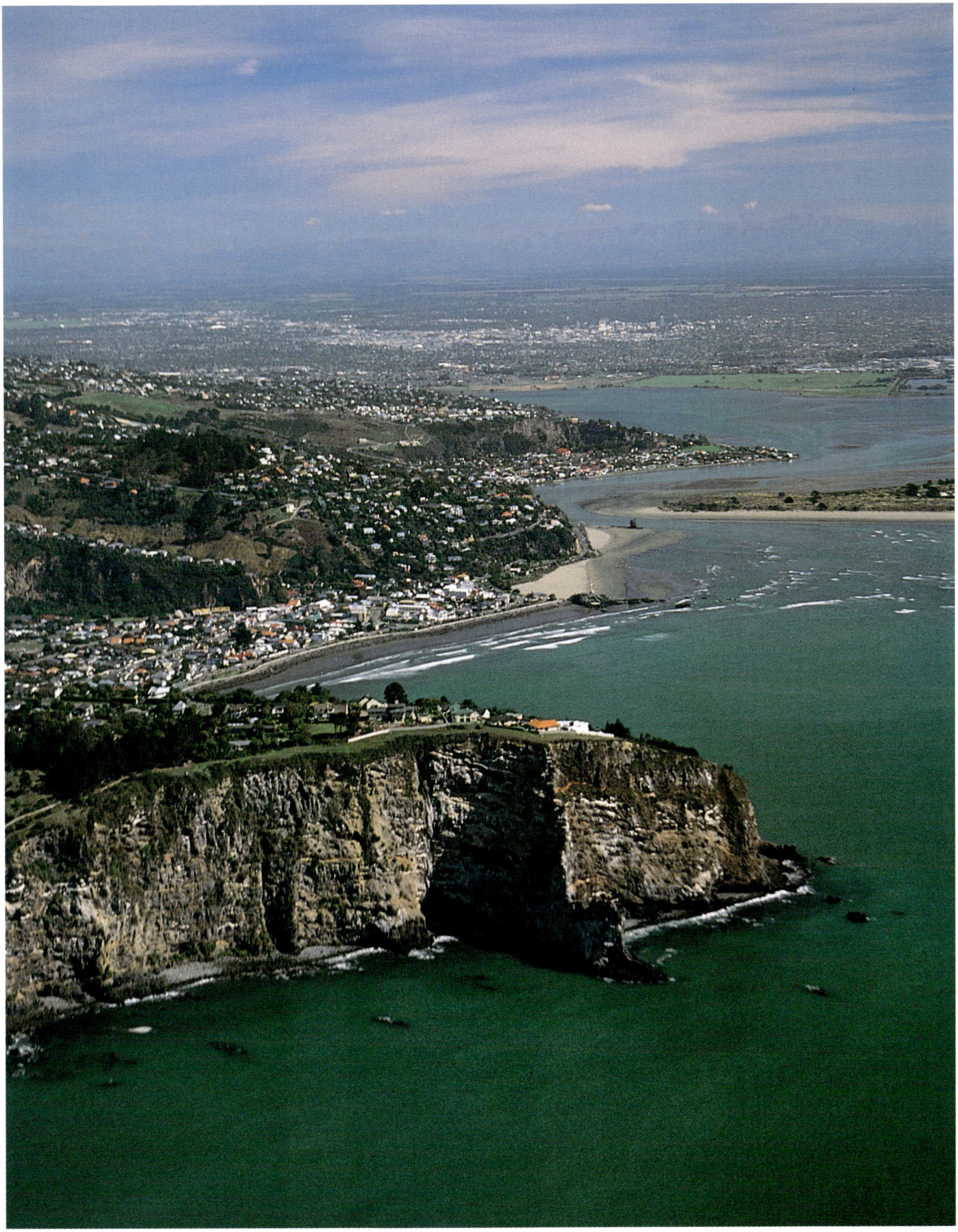

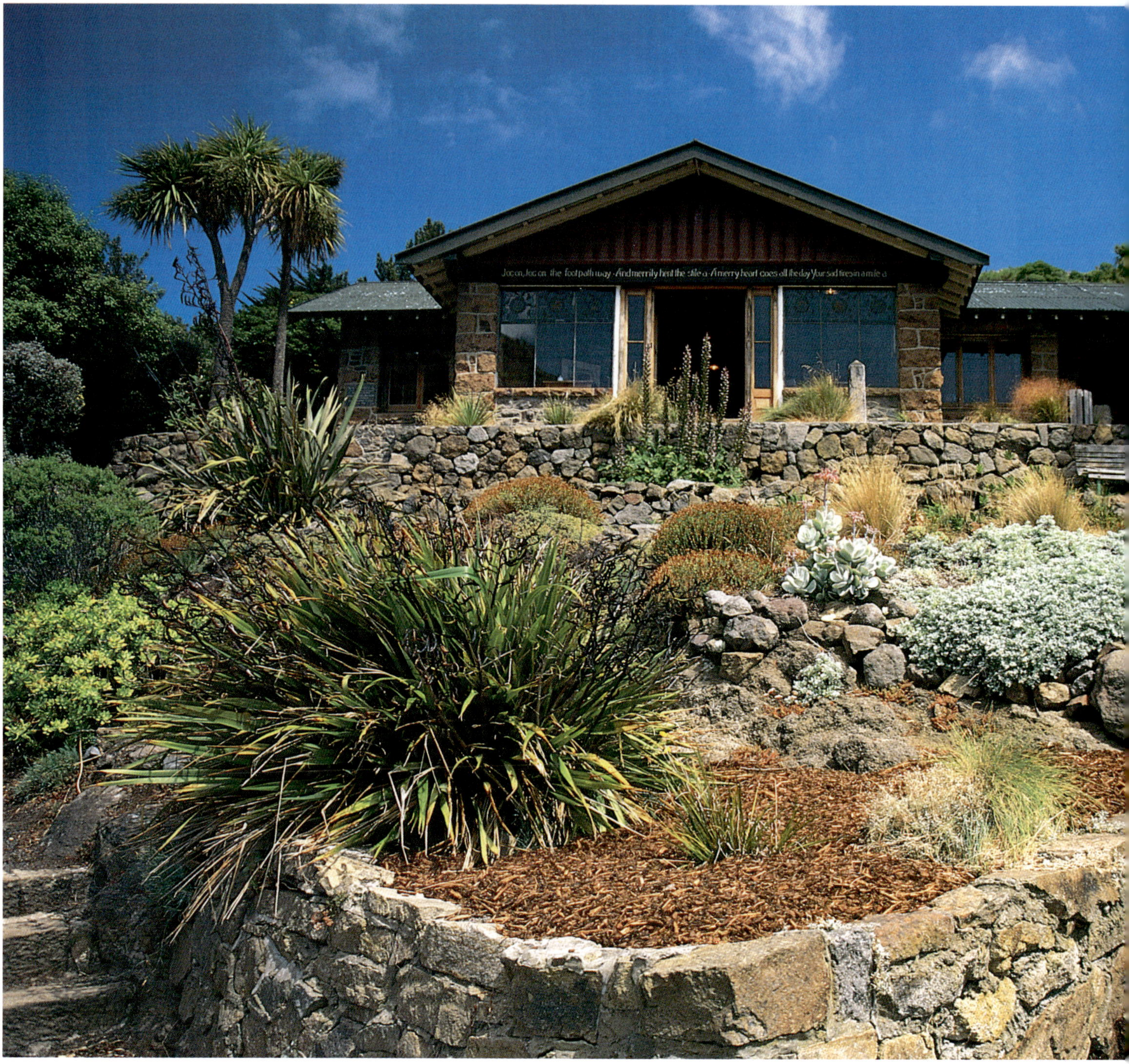

The Sign of the Kiwi was a roadhouse, opened in 1917. It is one of four that formed part of the vision of an early conservationist, Harry Ell. He wanted a series of reserves to be established along the Port Hills, linked by a summit road that would travel right across Banks Peninsula. The roadhouses were to offer shelter and refreshment. You can't stay there any longer, but the Sign of the Kiwi is now a tearoom. It's also an excellent starting point for many of the Port Hills walking routes.

The Port Hills, which form a backdrop to the city, remind us of Canterbury's volcanic past. They are a crater rim from the top of which are magnificent views down into Lyttelton Harbour or across to the Southern Alps. There are many walkways, pleasurable for the stunning views but also of great interest for the wide range of lichens and mosses that grow in the area. The hills are popular with mountain bikers and rock climbers.

When the first of the English settlers disembarked after their four-month sea voyage they had to walk over the Port Hills from Lyttelton. With children and worldly goods it was a long haul over the Bridle Path and down to Christchurch. These days there's a tunnel through the hills but the Bridle Path is still a popular walk for many locals.

The Sign of the Takahe is the first and most magnificent of Harry Ell's roadhouses. It was completed in 1948, an imposing neo-Gothic structure with wonderful views across to the Southern Alps. Today it houses a fine restaurant. Better roading and motor transport brought an end to Harry Ell's plan, but two other substantial roadhouses were built before that happened — the Sign of the Bellbird and the Sign of the Packhorse. Neither are used these days.

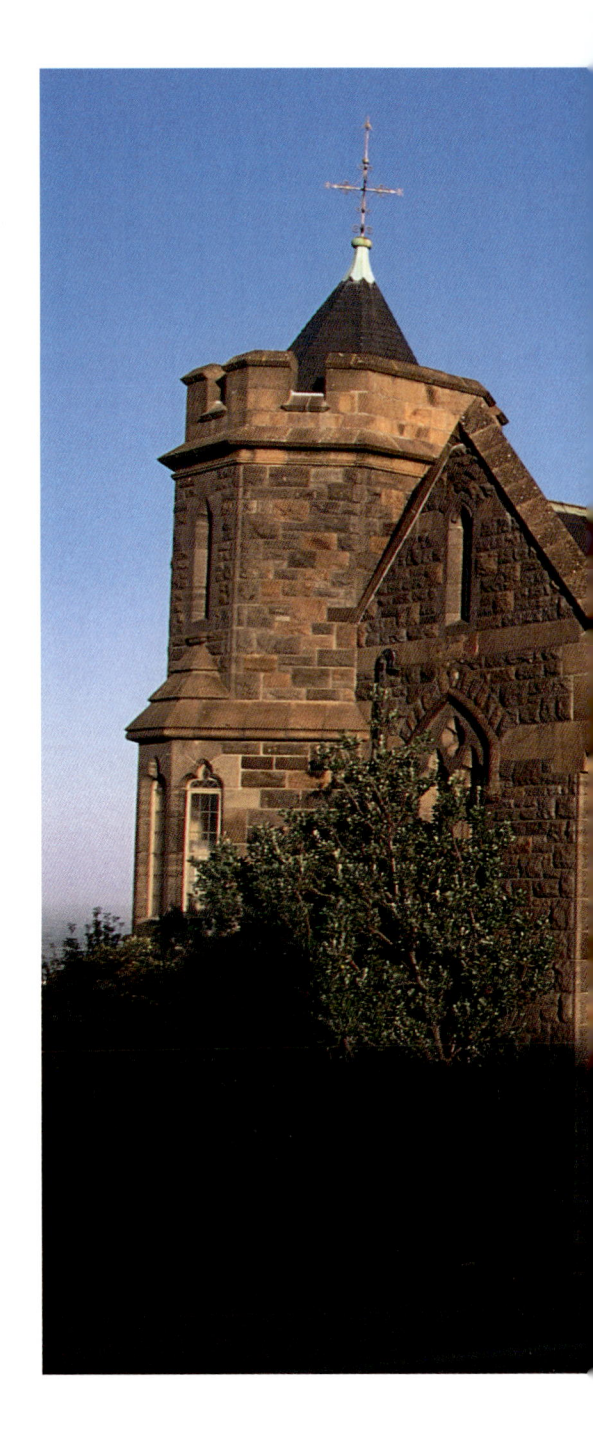

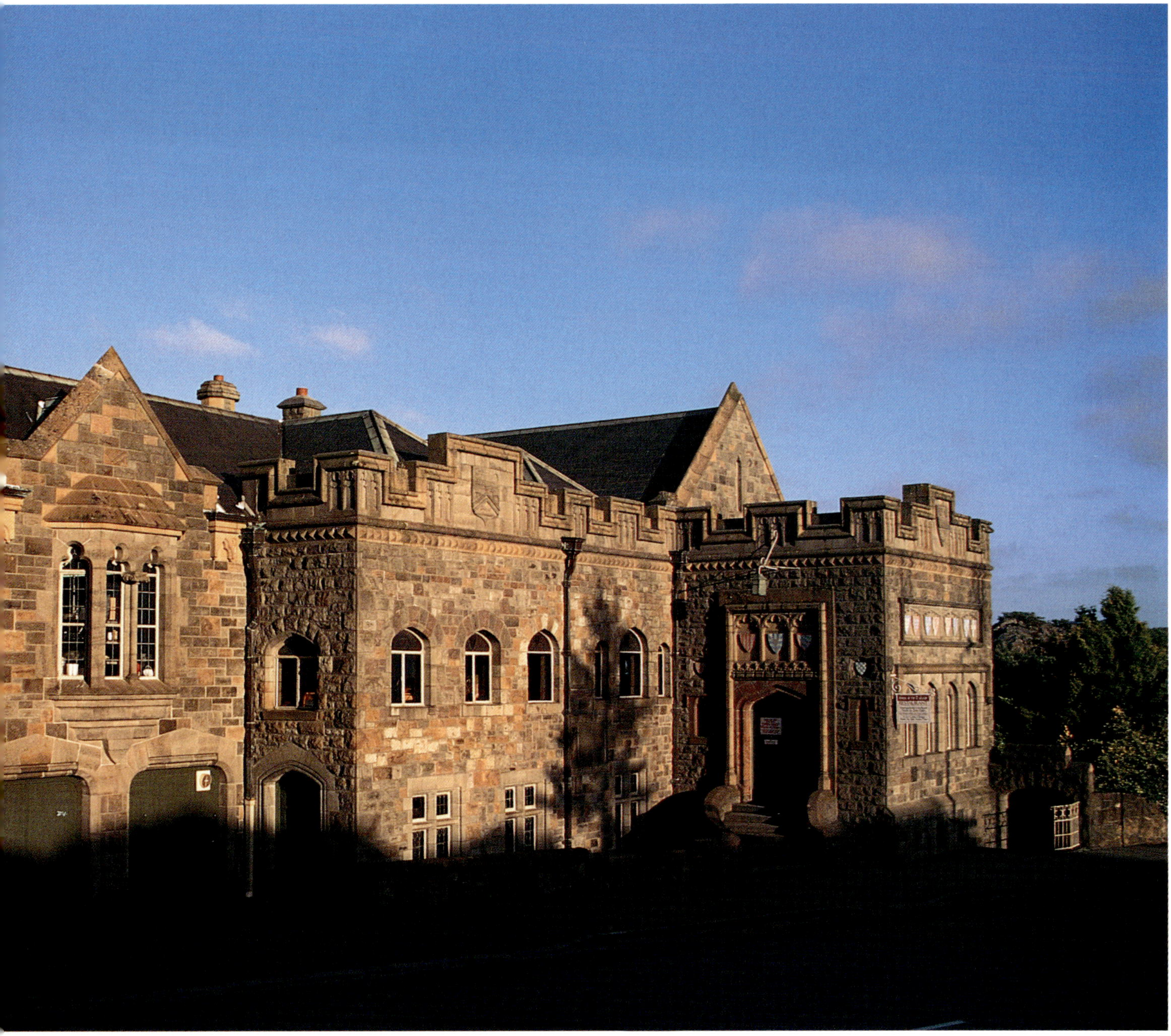

The Sign of the Takahe provides a fine night-time view as well as fine dining. There's something very appealing about overlooking the lights of a city at night.

Various features of the crater rim have been named and one of the most spectacular panoramas can be viewed from the top of Mt Cavendish. The Christchurch Gondola rides up from the Heathcote Valley to settle at the top station, which has been designed and landscaped to be as unobtrusive as possible in this area of native reserve. As well as a restaurant and café, there is a Time Tunnel which graphically illustrates the history of Banks Peninsula from the dawn of time to the present day.

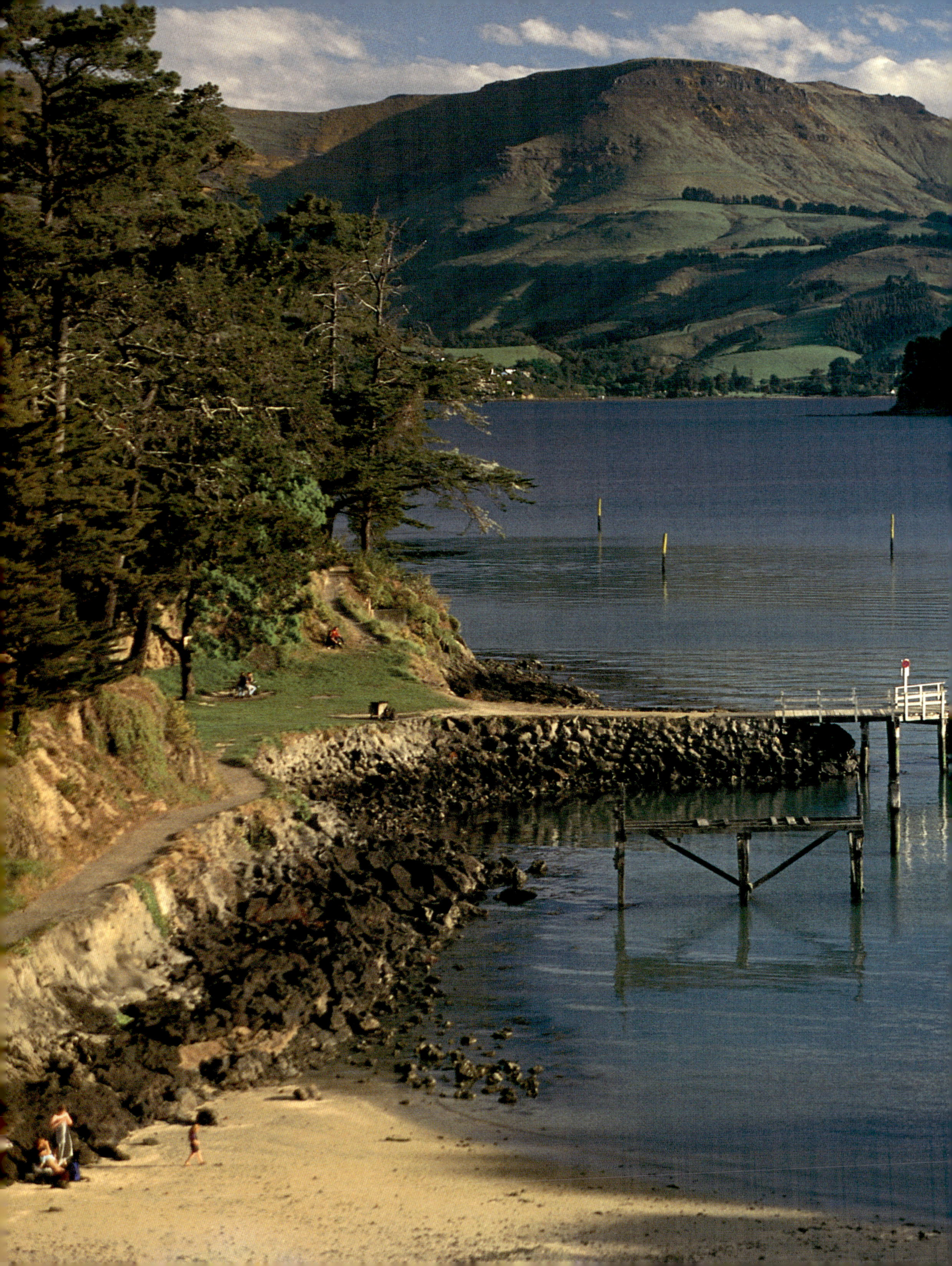

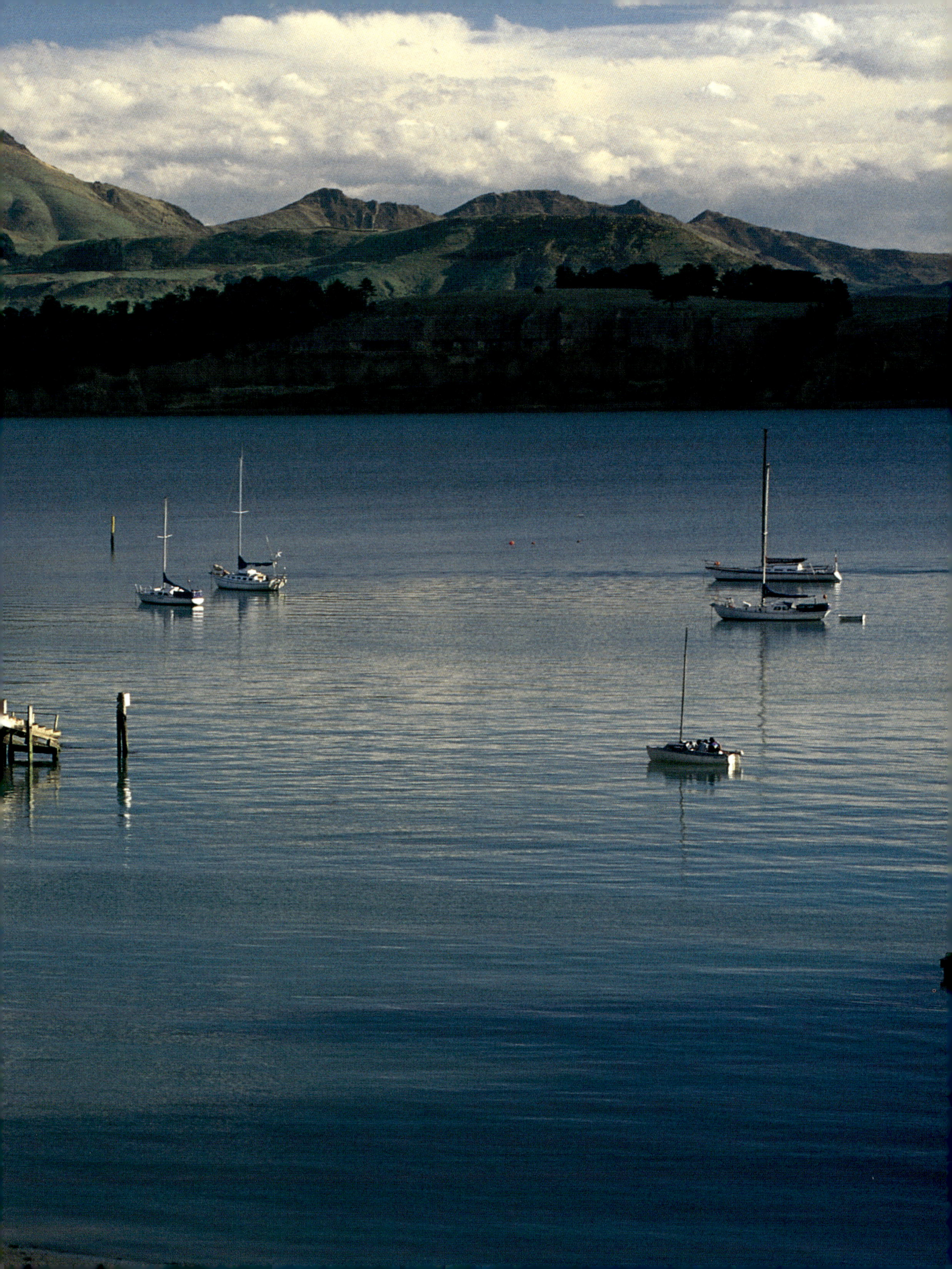

Lyttelton is very much a working port but the harbour also offers many recreational opportunities. There are plenty of pubs, restaurants and cafés in which to share the day's stories of sailing or windsurfing or exploration of two of the islands in the harbour – Ripapa and Quail – both of which have interesting and varied histories.

Previous page: Lyttelton Harbour was the port of entry for the English settlers and was given its present name in honour of Lord Lyttelton, who was the Chairman of the Canterbury Association. However Maori, who had lived on Banks Peninsula for many centuries, called it Te Whaka-raupo – the harbour of the bulrush reeds.

Until the opening of the road tunnel under the Port Hills, Lyttelton was serviced by rail. The rail tunnel was completed in 1867, the first in the world to be drilled through volcanic rock. The signal box (above) remaining from those early days has been preserved and is a fine example. The finials are particularly worthy of note: in line with 14th century practice, they were believed to offer protection from witches.

Lyttelton's Timeball Station was built in 1875 and is still in working order, although it was supplanted by radio signals as the port's time-keeper in 1934. Before that, at 1.00pm every day, it signalled Greenwich Mean Time to all the ships in the harbour by dropping the Timeball.

There are two cemeteries in Lyttelton. The first was for the early English settlers who stayed in the port and who were Anglican; the second was for 'others' and includes seven unmarked graves of prisoners who had been hanged in Lyttelton's gaol.

Sunrise over Lyttelton Harbour. The harbour is an old volcanic crater, the legacy of an eruption that occurred 11 million years ago.

The moon, Saturn and Venus shine out over Christchurch.

Onawe is a peninsula jutting out into Akaroa Harbour. There is a pleasant walk up to the trig station at its summit, with great views out to the Heads and over the surrounding hills. In the early 1800s it was the site of a Maori pa, or fortified village, and is notable in the history of the major South Island tribe – Ngai Tahu – for a massacre of their people in 1832 by the North Island warrior Te Rauparaha and his war party.

Akaroa (Maori for long harbour) is one of the delightful harbours of Banks Peninsula, which was named after the noted botanist Joseph Banks who as a young man travelled with Captain James Cook on his first voyage of discovery. Banks' observations and exquisite drawings make a wonderful early record of New Zealand. When Cook charted the coastline of New Zealand one of the mistakes he made was to assume that this 'bump' off the east coast of Te Wai Pounamu (the South Island) was not connected to the mainland. A survey in 1809 showed it was in fact a peninsula.

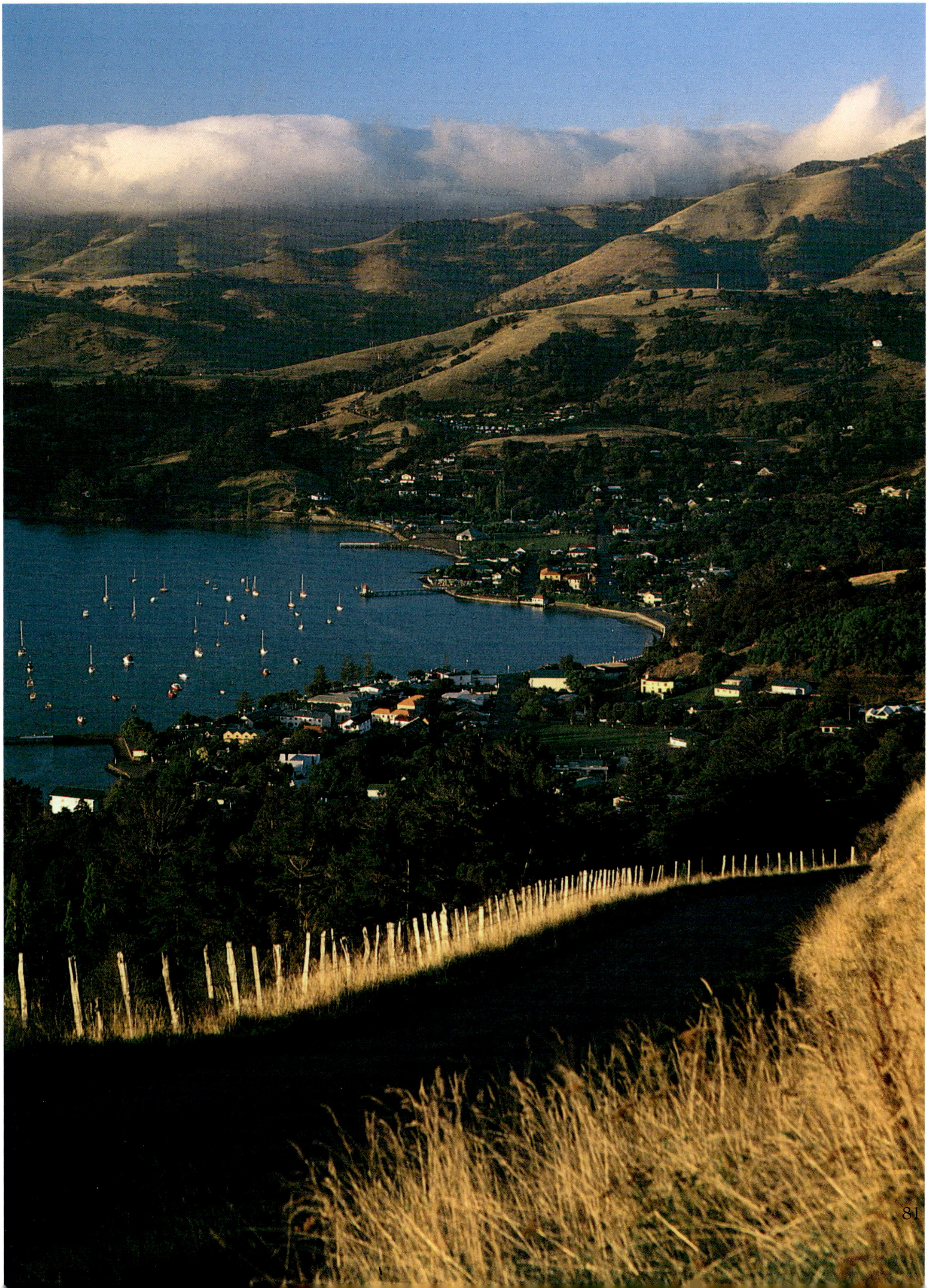

Mucking about in boats of one kind and another is very much part of Akaroa's recreational scene, but just a stroll along the waterfront can be very pleasant.

Akaroa has a commercial fishing fleet as well. And there's nothing quite as tasty as some fresh local cod bought at Daly's Wharf.

There is a French flavour to the settlement of Akaroa that can be traced back to 1838 when Captain Jean Langlois, a French whaler, paid a group of local Maori 6000 francs for 30,000 acres.

Langlois returned to France to request government support to colonise New Zealand. Too late! By the time Langlois and a group of 63 settlers returned, the Treaty of Waitangi had been signed and British sovereignty had been established.

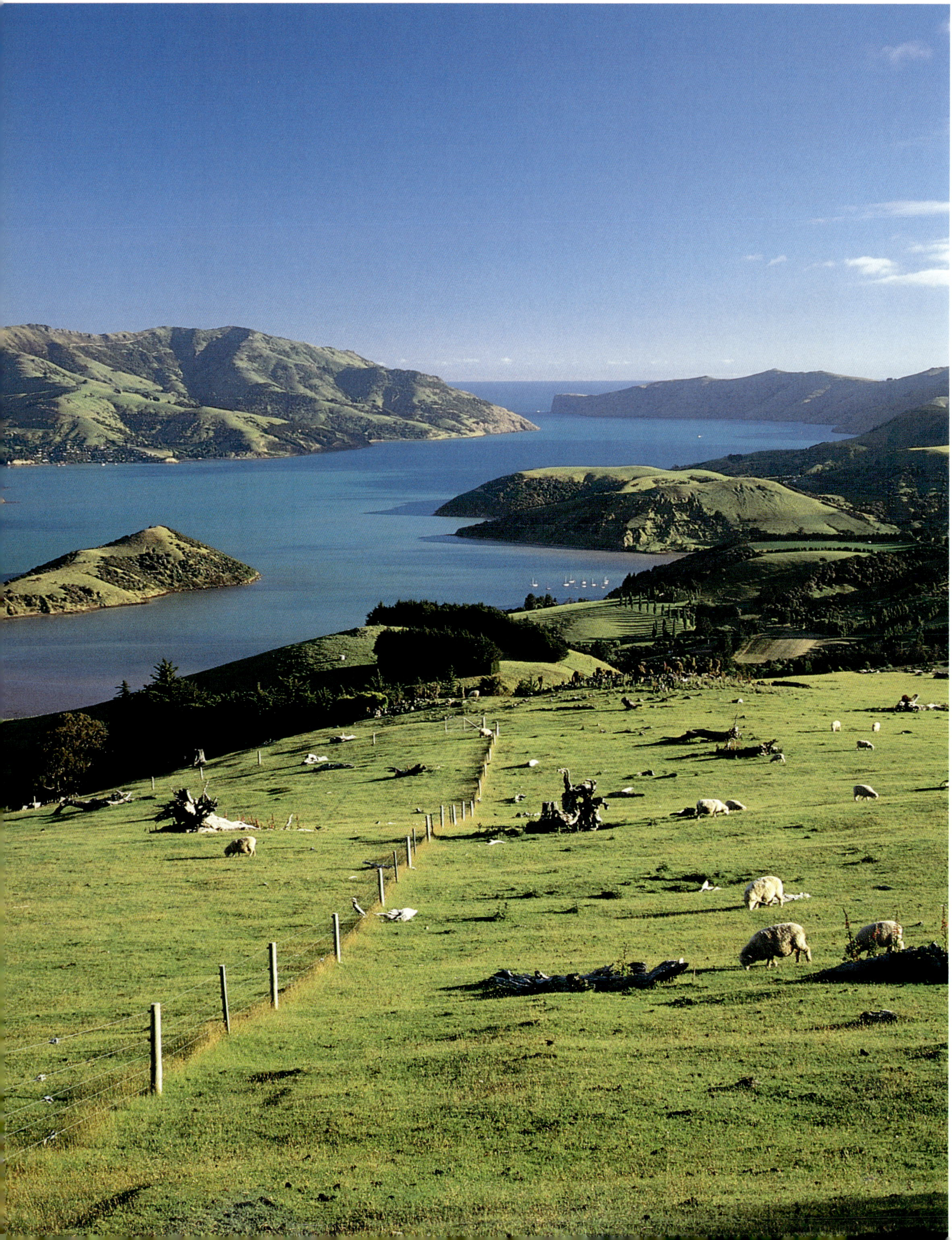

The main activity on Banks Peninsula is farming, but it now has a fledgling wine producing industry as well. The beauty of the area has also attracted a sizeable community of artists and craftspeople. Wildlife and sea birds, too, are a feature of the harbour area; they include the playful Hector's dolphin (above), found only in New Zealand waters and the smallest of the world's oceanic dolphins, and the little blue penguin, the world's smallest penguin.

Rugged mountains, native bush and swamps met the early inhabitants of Canterbury; for the English settlers it must have taken determination to hold onto those dreams of pastures new. But those who persevered turned the Canterbury Plains into one of the most productive and prosperous farming areas of the country.

These hay fields, seen in South Canterbury, show just one aspect of the region's agricultural diversity. Cropping, dairy farming, sheep, cattle and deer have now been joined by wine production as major contributors to the region's prosperity.

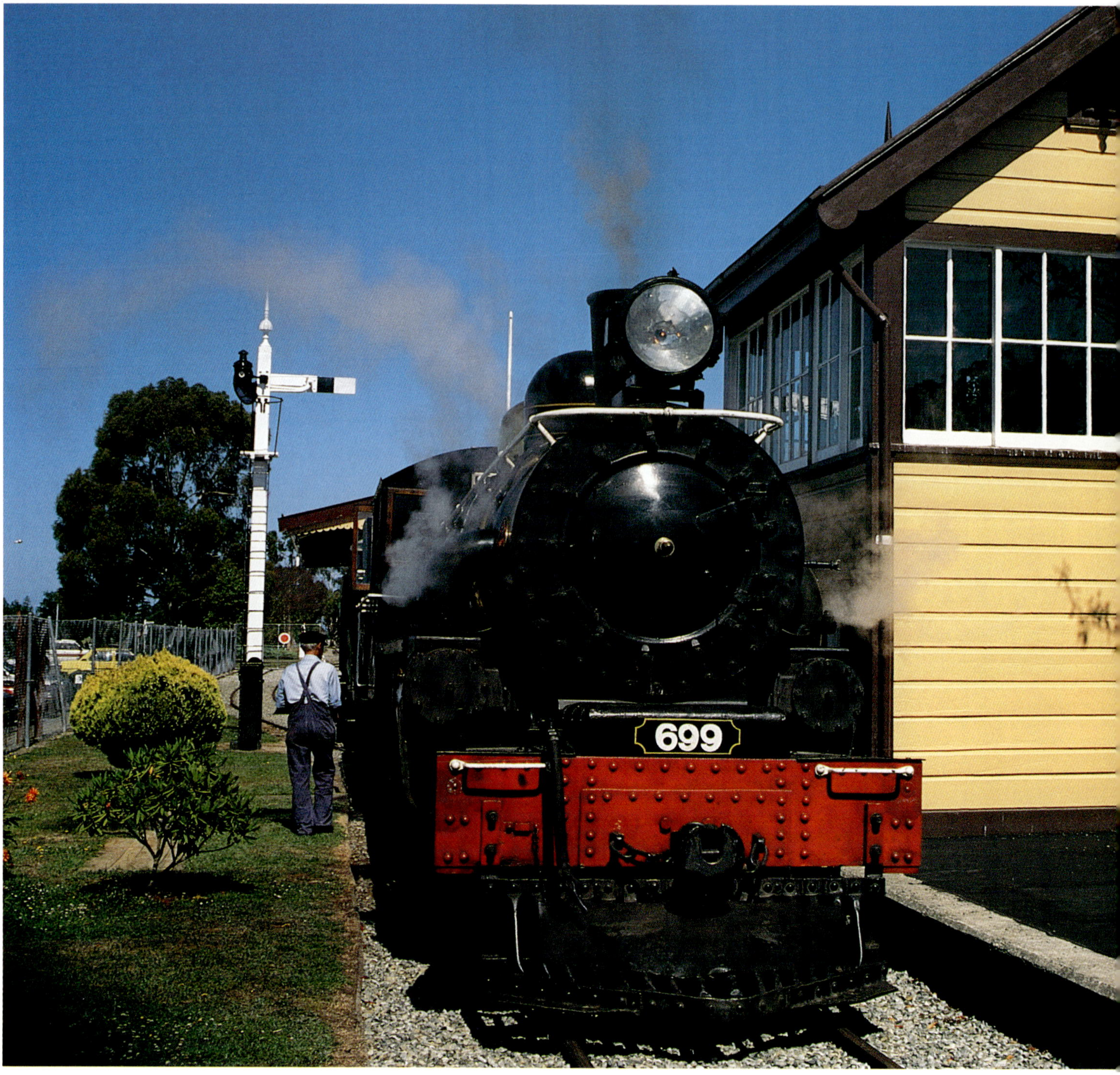
699

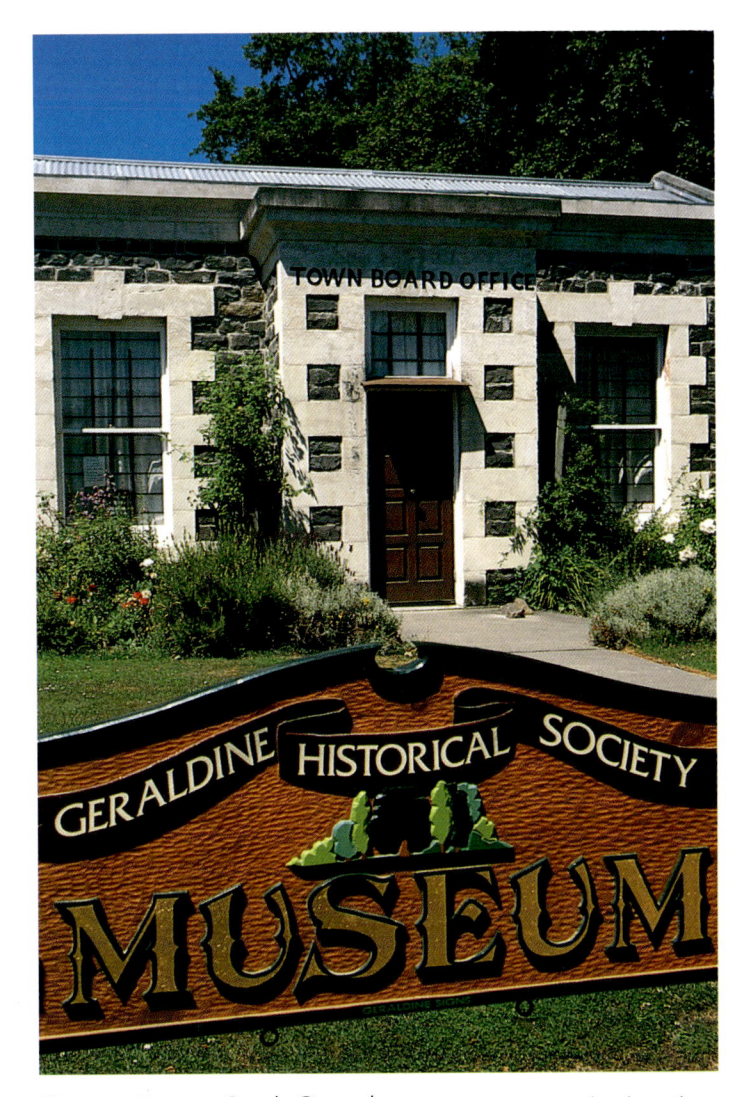

Pleasant Point in South Canterbury was once a major junction but now is best known for its railway museum (left). Its glorious old steam trains get regular outings on the three kilometres of line that exist as part of the museum complex.

Not far away, in the small farming centre of Geraldine, there is a museum (above) that houses artefacts from the early pioneering days.

The Sacred Heart Basilica is a handsome landmark in Canterbury's southern city, Timaru. Built on the gentle hills that mark the end of the Canterbury Plains, Timaru draws much of its prosperity from the farming and forestry of the district. Its popular Caroline Bay is one of the safest swimming beaches in New Zealand; Maori called it Te Maru, 'the place of shelter', the only one for travellers canoeing along this coastline.

In his day Richard Pearse, a local farmer, was called 'Mad Pearse'. Now Timaru's airport is named after him. Just a little further north, near the town of Temuka, there is a memorial to him (above). Others may challenge the claim, but South Canterbury people maintain that Pearse managed to stay airborne for 100 yards in his homemade aircraft on 3 March 1903. That means he beat the Wright brothers to be the first in the world to achieve powered flight.

Lake Coleridge (above), in mid-Canterbury, a long glacier lake surrounded by the Southern Alps, is the site of the first large-scale hydroelectric project in New Zealand, which began generating power in 1914. More importantly for fly fishers, the lake is a very popular destination for those who hanker after rainbow or brown trout. Braided riverbeds like this one on the right can be seen throughout the South Island. The various channels can accommodate a river's many moods throughout the year.

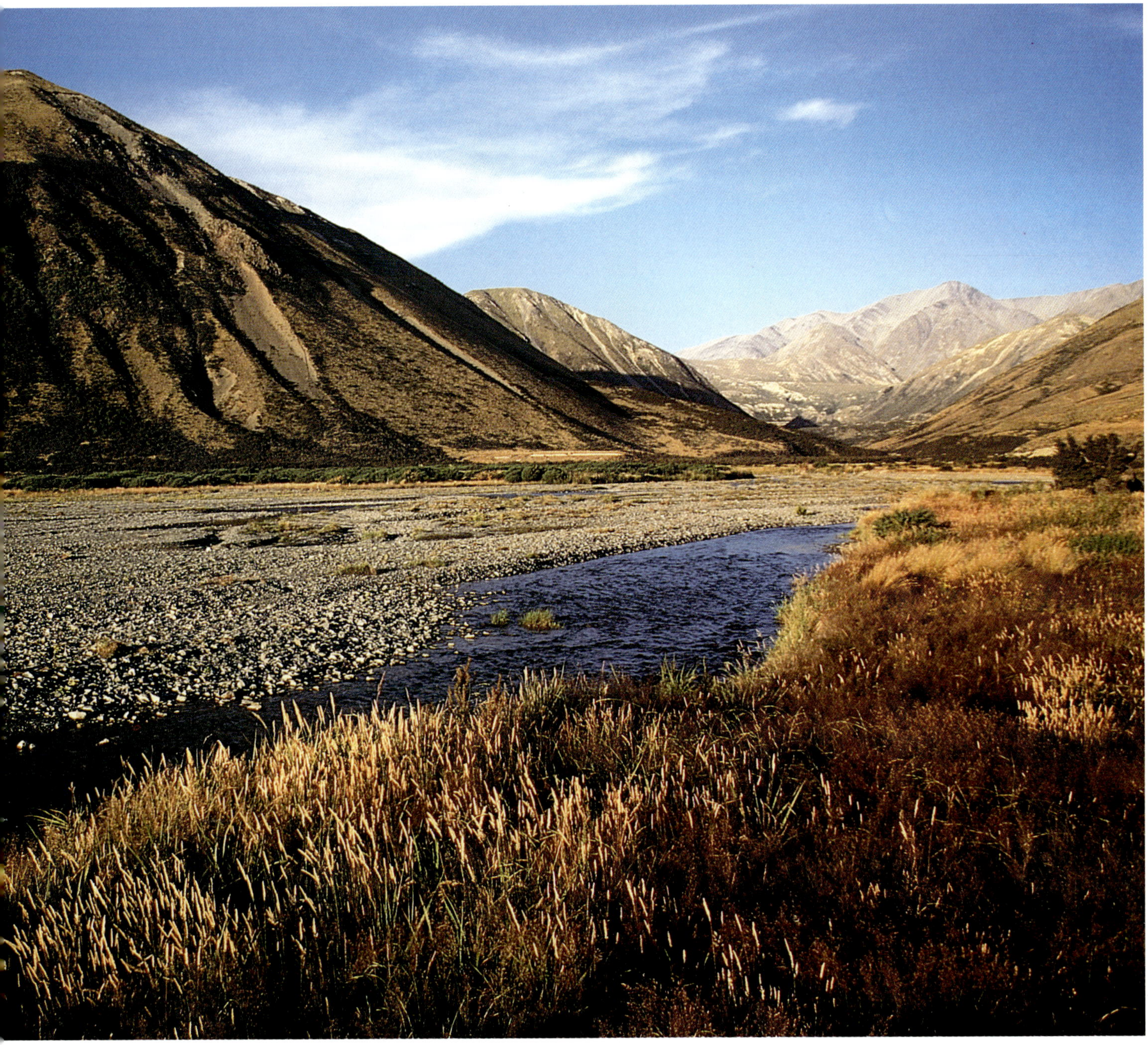

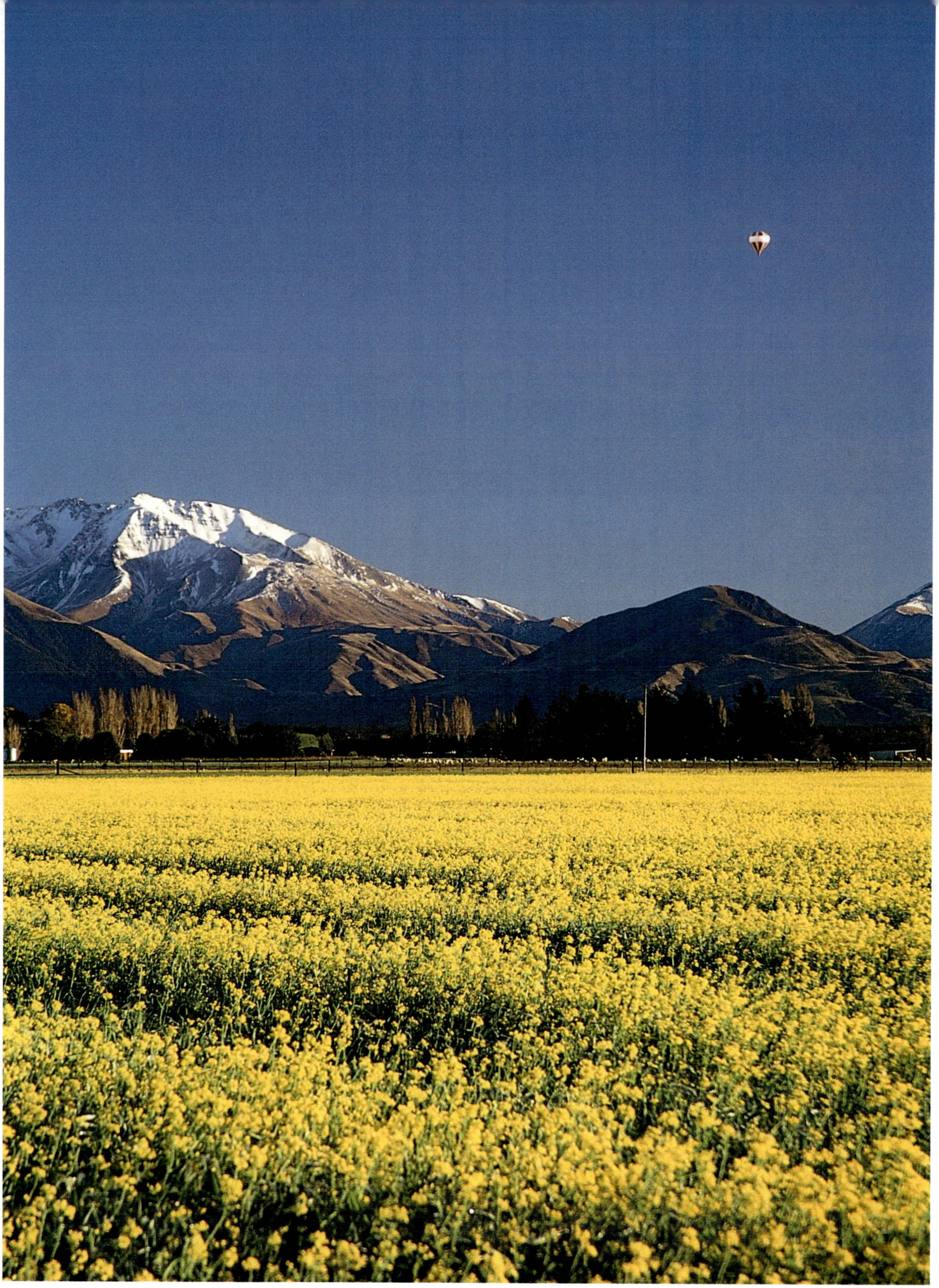

The Southern Alps, which form a spine down the middle of the South Island, are spectacularly beautiful. It is magic to see them from the basket of a hot air balloon, set against a field of rapeseed and the tiny village of Methven (left) that snuggles into the foothills. The mountains provide great outdoor opportunities: skiing at Mt Hutt, or bush tramping and mountain climbing in the beautiful wilderness area of Arthur's Pass National Park.

Each year there is a curiously large number of people willing to take up the extraordinary challenge of getting from one side of the South Island to the other – by running over the mountains, kayaking down the Waimakariri River and cycling across the plains to Christchurch. The Speight's Coast to Coast has become internationally famous and is one of the toughest such challenges in the world.

There are certainly easier ways to get a thrill out of Canterbury's braided rivers, and an alpine jetboat is one of them. River rafting has also become a very popular activity in the region – and the white-water kayaking doesn't have to be competitive!

99

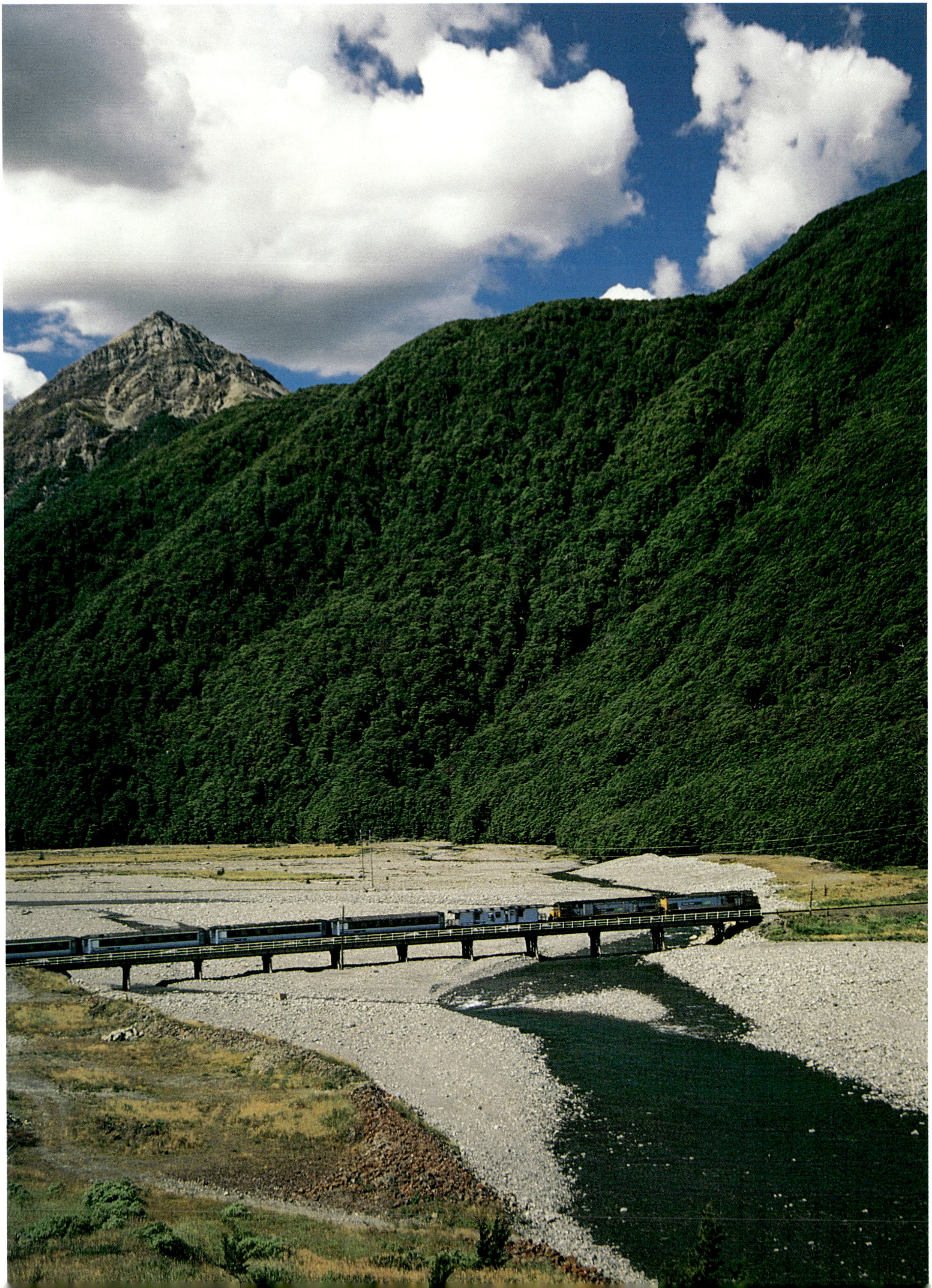

The Castle Hill Conservation area is of particular interest for its limestone formations, the tallest of these, at the top of the hill, being around 10 metres high. Charred moa bones and rock drawings are evidence of early Maori using the area, probably for shelter.

Arthur's Pass is one of the three passes over the Southern Alps and it is still the only rail link between the east and west coasts. It is named after Arthur Dudley Dobson, a surveyor, engineer and early explorer who was told of the existence of the pass by the Maori chief Tarapuhi. Before the railway was opened in 1923, this magnificent but potentially treacherous route was serviced by a stagecoach, which made the journey twice a week. These days the TranzAlpine offers much greater comfort.

The Hurunui Hotel was granted its first licence in 1860. The licence has never lapsed and the hotel is one of the oldest in the country. Travellers on the main route between Canterbury and Nelson, in the north of the South Island, had to cross the Hurunui River; when it flooded people could be held up for days, so the hotel added an accommodation house in 1864.

In the early days there were frequent drownings in the river and a morgue was kept at the back of the premises. After a great flood in 1868 – when the river flowed a mile wide, according to contemporary accounts – the hotel was relocated to its present site near the bridge. Made of limestone blocks held together and lined on the inside with a mixture of clay, tussock and lime, the hotel and the original stables, now a gift shop (above), make a very pleasant place to stop for refreshments.

Overleaf: The Hurunui District encompasses a wonderful variety of landscapes, from the beech forests of the Southern Alps to the vineyards of the Waipara Valley and a coastline that borders the Pacific Ocean. Gore Bay, seen here, is safe for swimming and good for surfing, and is a popular holiday spot. With a High Gothic Revival touch of their own, the spectacular cliffs of siltstone that are such a feature of the area are known as the 'Cathedrals'.

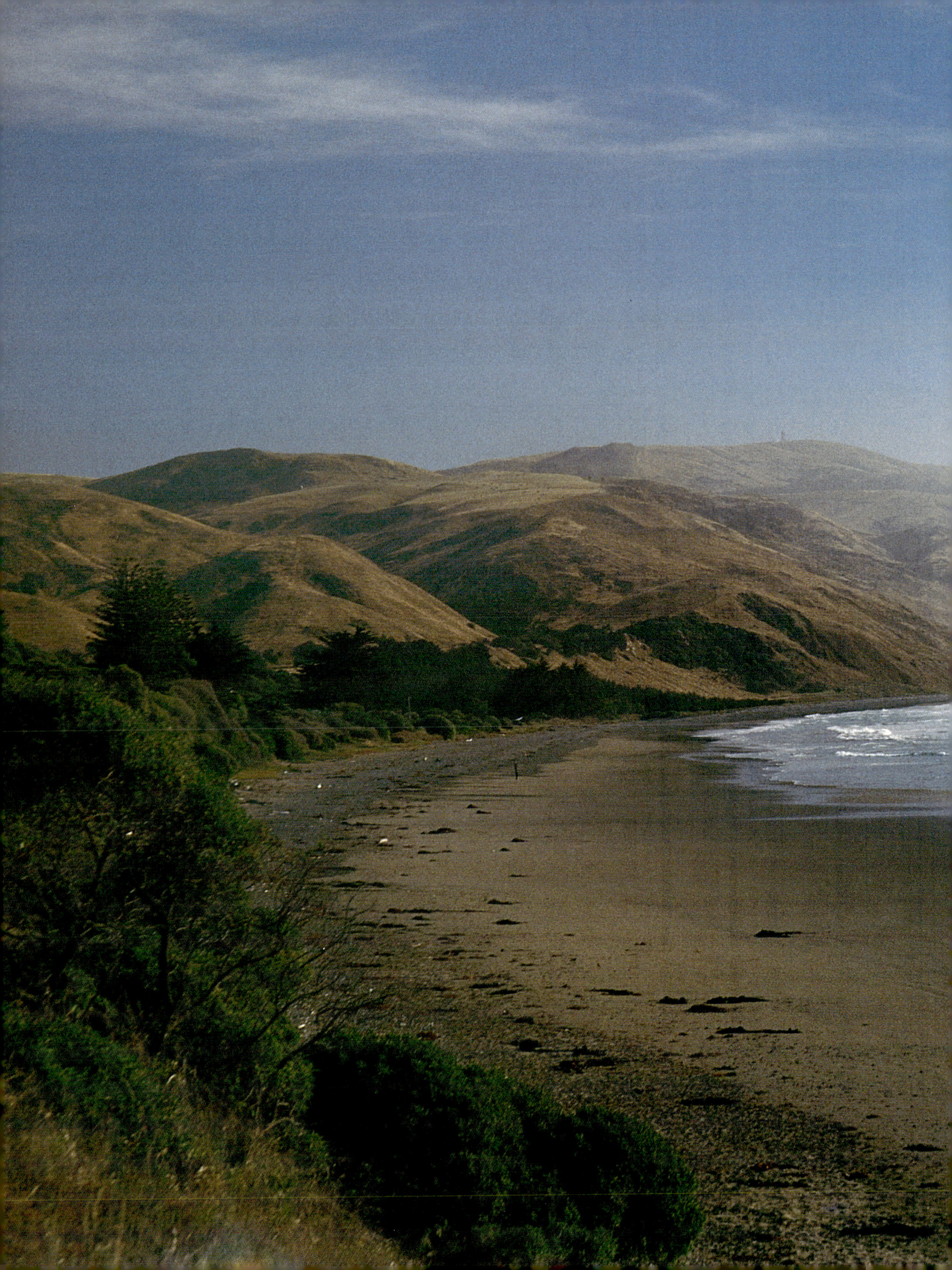

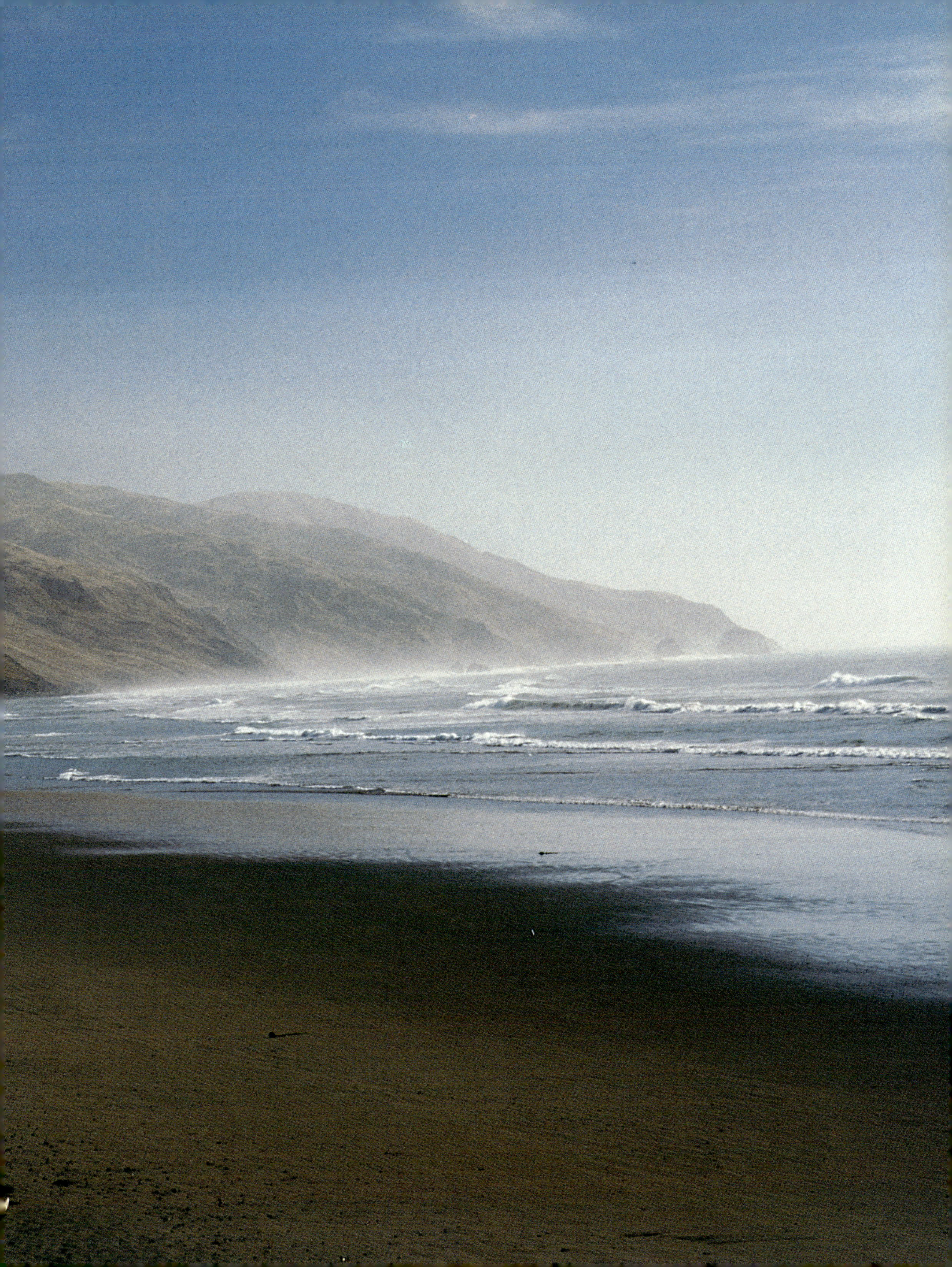

These days North Canterbury is a delight to travel through, but it used to be much tougher. The historic Ferry Bridge over the Waiau River was completed in 1887, after the local community had existed for 13 years without a bridge. On the day it was officially opened there was a great party and a marquee was set up on the flat land beside the river: to this day it is still called Champagne Flat.

Like the rest of the province, North Canterbury has proved to be a prosperous farming area. Traditionally this was sheep and dairy farming country, but now some areas are turning out some very fine wines.

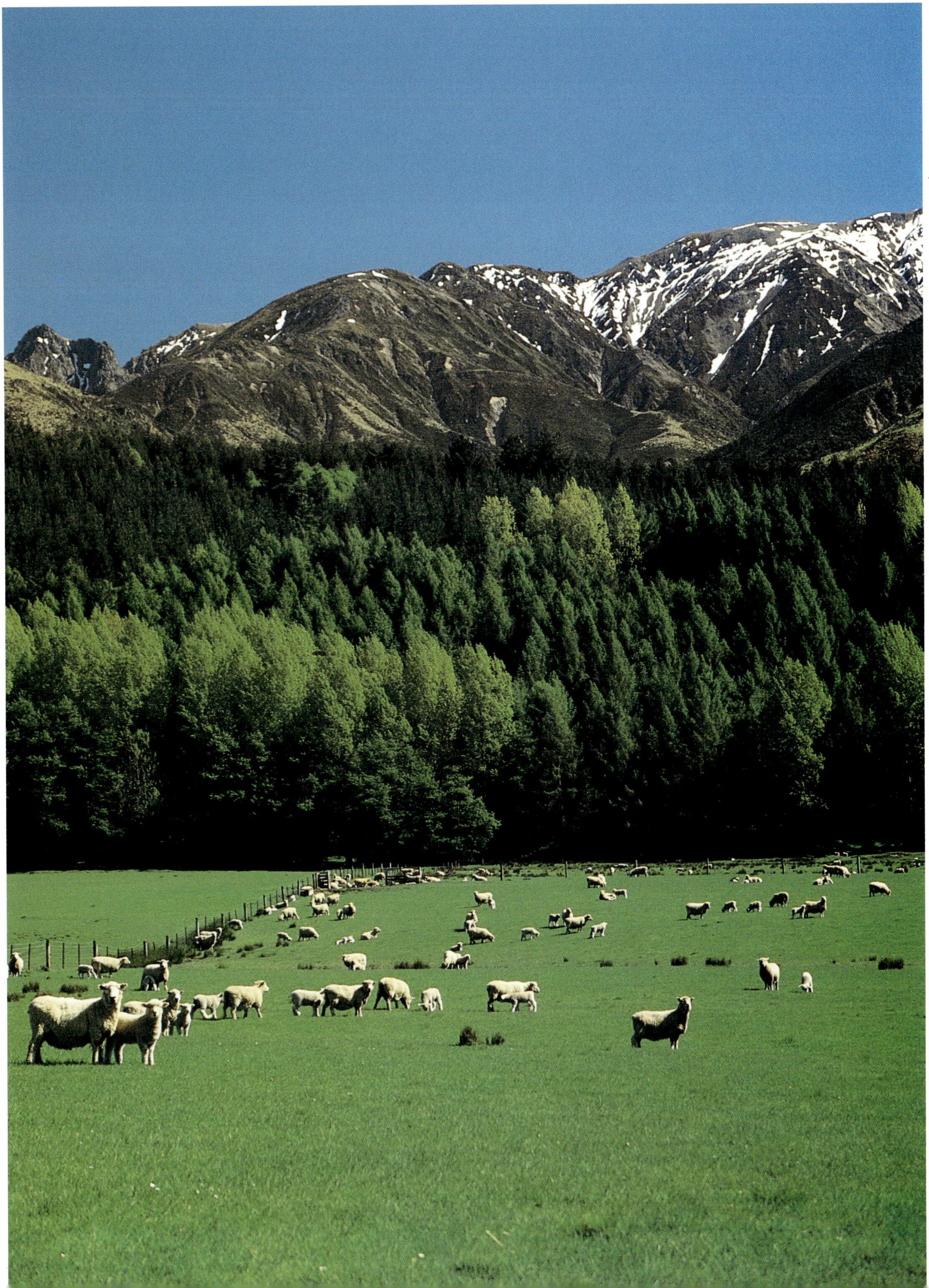

Hanmer Springs is an alpine village with hot thermal springs. In summer and winter, there are beautiful walks through exotic forests and native bush, horse trekking, and rafting or kayaking on the Waiau River; and of course there's skiing in winter. But whatever time of the year there are the hot pools to soak away the aches of the day – or just to laze in!

One wouldn't expect to come across ostriches in North Canterbury, but farming these unusual-looking birds is becoming a popular alternative to the region's more traditional activities.

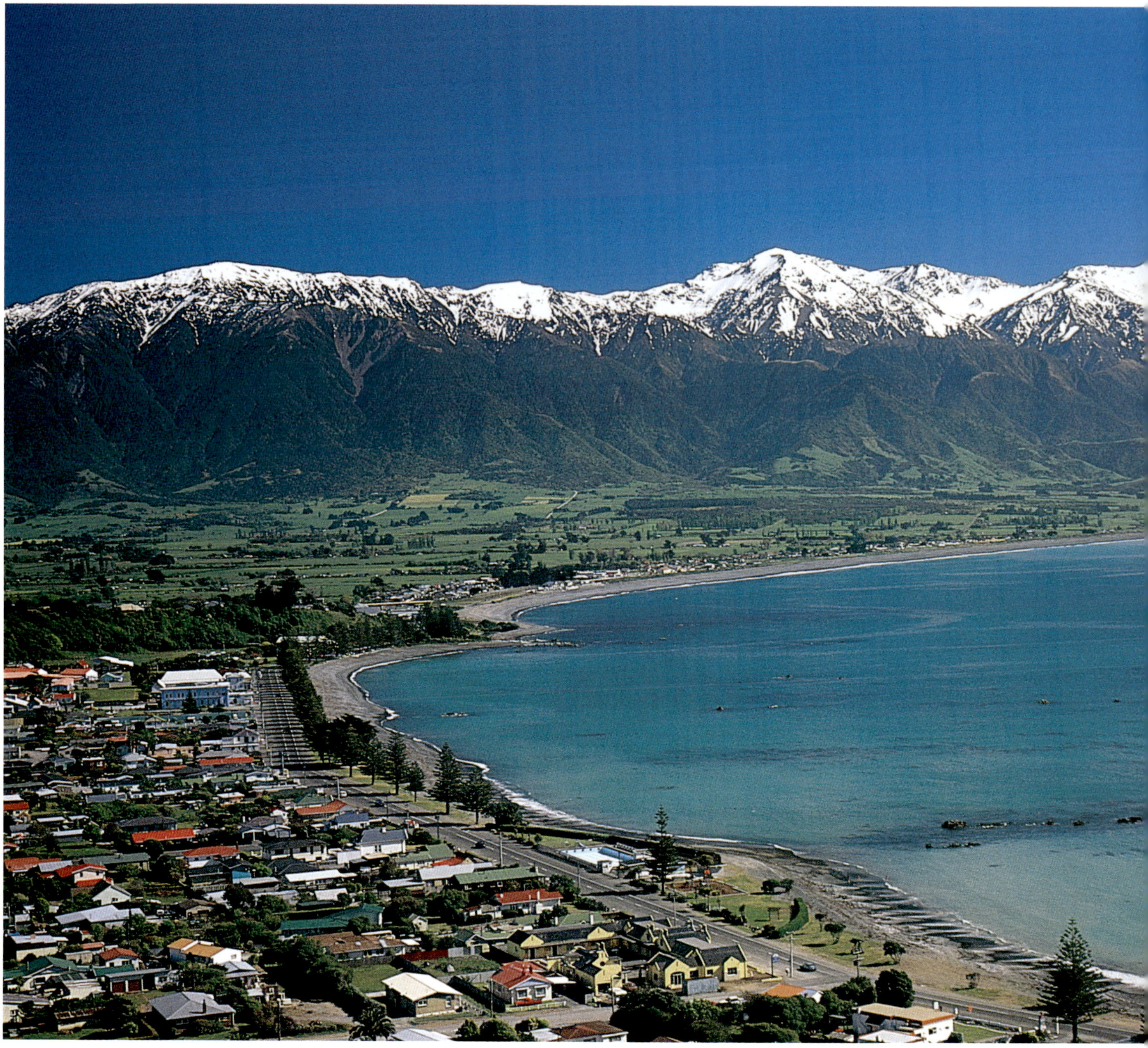

Kaikoura, approximately 180 kilometres north of Christchurch, offers another of those unusual juxtapositions – the sea and snow-clad mountains almost cheek by jowl. The little township is on the rocky peninsula that juts out from the farmland of the foothills. But it is the waters off this peninsula that provide a rich habitat for marine animals and seabirds and from which the Maori name originates; Kaikoura means 'a meal of crayfish'.

Overleaf: Fishing is still important to the area, but what brings visitors to Kaikoura today is the opportunity to swim with the intelligent and playful dolphins or to see close at hand fur seals or a variety of whales – the most magnificent of these being the sperm whale.

First published in 1999 by New Holland Kowhai
an imprint of New Holland Publishers (NZ) Ltd
Auckland • Sydney • London • Cape Town

218 Lake Road, Northcote, Auckland, New Zealand
14 Aquatic Drive, Frenchs Forest, NSW 2086, Australia
86–88 Edgware Road, London W2 2EA, United Kingdom
80 McKenzie Street, Cape Town 8001, South Africa

Copyright © 1999 in text: Liz Grant
Copyright © 1999 in photography: David Wall with the exception
of Andrew Fear: page 49; Tony Harrington: page 97 (top)
Copyright © 1999 New Holland Publishers (NZ) Ltd

ISBN: 1-877246-25-5

A catalogue record for this book is available
from the National Library of New Zealand

Managing Editor: Matt Turner
Design: Chris O'Brien

3 5 7 9 10 8 6 4 2

Colour reproduction by Pica Digital, Singapore
Printed by Times Offset (M) Sdn Bhd

All rights reserved. No part of this publication may be reproduced,
stored in a retrieval system, or transmitted in any form or by any means,
electronic, mechanical, photocopying, recording or otherwise,
without the prior permission of the publishers and copyright holders.

Half title page: *Chalice*, Cathedral Square
Pages 2–3: Arthur's Pass Road